The Purpose and the Power of the Average Church

Has your church plateaued or has it reached its God honoring potential?

by
Pastor Jack Eldred

Contents

Introduction

Average:

1. an arithmetic mean.

2. a typical or usual amount, rate, or level.

3. of or forming an average.

4. not unusual, common.[i]

I realize that the word *average* is sort of frowned upon in America. Nobody wants to be just *average*; we all want to be exceptional. And we pastors want our churches to be exceptional, too. Too often, we think that "exceptional" means "big." But the fact is that most churches in America are average-sized, not large—though that doesn't mean they're not exceptional!

Something that is small or average-sized can still be tremendously important. Just think of your own body and how many different parts God put in it. Besides two legs, two arms, a head, and a trunk, most of the other pieces are small—small, but very necessary for our health. Most of us are somewhere near the average height and weight, but we don't take offense at that. Why? We are human beings, made in the image of God, fearfully and wonderfully made to the specification of our Creator. And after much thought and reflection, I believe that the average church has been birthed and put together by the specifications of Creator God, too. A few mega churches, a few large churches, and a majority of small churches is how God chooses to manifest His body to the world.

I'm glad we don't evaluate people by size, the way we evaluate our churches. Can you imagine if every time you stood in a group you were valued by your height? Imagine, for example, if you applied for a job for which fifteen other people were applying and the interviewers called you in, made you take off your shoes, and measured each person—and then gave the job to the tallest person. That's crazy, isn't it? And so is putting so much emphasis on church attendance numbers.

The power of the Church is not in sheer numbers. It's in each congregation offering their gifts and talents up to God and using them within their respective calling and community, becoming salt and light and the living body of Christ to a dark and lost world.

This book is not an anti–church-growth book, but it is about learning how to never stress over numbers again. It is about learning how to grow in a way that is natural for you and your church. So get ready to have your thinking challenged about how you see yourself and your church.

And because I know that it pains us to be thought of as average, I won't use the term "average church" but will instead refer to the average church as the "small church." Of course, I'm not sure *that* term is much easier for people to digest!

To the Small Church Pastors

To all the ministers who pastor the small church, this book is for you. Thank you for your tenacity, dedication, and love. You may not recognize what a giant you are in God's army, but as a pastor of a small church for twenty-five years, I recognize it. I celebrate you, your leaders, and all of your members who make up your church, which is a vital part of the body of Christ here on earth. And remember, the small church is how God reveals Himself to most of the world.

You are the body of Christ to a specific part of the planet, and there is none other on the planet just like you. No other church has been placed exactly where God placed you and your church, and God put you there because He needs you there—to be salt and light to your particular area. Whether you are in rural America or an inner city or somewhere in between, you have been handpicked by your

Heavenly Father to make disciples and be His hands extended to your part of the world.

If you have been struggling with not being able to grow your church to record proportions, it could take a while for you to process this, but I believe that God is well pleased with you and your current church attendance. This thinking that the church should continually break attendance records can be attributed to a handful of mega churches who are held up as a model of how church should be done, and it has created a church culture that is, in my opinion, neither realistic nor healthy. The one percent who pastor mega churches are certainly something to marvel at, but statistics show that 99 percent of us were not ordained to do that. What we *can* do and have been ordained to do is grow to our God-honoring potential. And when we do that we will hear our Heavenly Father say, "Well done, good and faithful servant!"

Listen carefully to what I'm about to tell you: don't let numbers, or lack of them, discourage you. God's mandate does not require numbers, but it does require love. So, keep loving God with all of your heart, mind, strength, and soul, and keep loving people, *all* people. We learn so much when we love all types of people and take the time to listen and share experiences with them.

And in the midst of all of this loving, don't forget to love yourself. Rest on purpose. Have fun on purpose. Relax on purpose. Take time to enjoy the world that God gave you. Look at your daily planner and see if *you* are on there, see if your *family* is on there, see if *fun* is on there, and see if *God* is on there—really!

Finally, keep on being who God called you to be: a leader of the most powerful and purpose-filled institution on the planet, the Church.

Thanks!

Reality Check: Has Your Church Reached a Plateau— or its God-honoring Potential?

We have come to use the word *plateau* when a church cannot produce perpetual growth. What do you think when you hear the word *plateau?* If you are a pastor or church leader, chances are you cringe, because it is a reminder that you haven't added any significant numbers to your flock lately.

Now, what do you think about when you hear this phrase: "You have reached your God-honoring potential"? Maybe you think about hitting the mark or firing on all cylinders. Most of the pastors I know do their best to hit the mark and fire on all cylinders. They do their best to live up to their God-honoring potential, which will most likely produce the size church that they are ordained to lead.

What God and Nature Teach Us about Growth

I believe the Bible and nature itself teach that everything that is normal and healthy will grow to its natural height, width, and depth if given a healthy environment.

Most people will reach their maximum height by their late teens to early twenties, and they don't feel bad or guilty about not growing another inch. In our academic lives, too, we are often content to reach a "plateau." I, like most pastors I know, am a life-long learner, but at some point most of us are satisfied and feel we have reached a God-honoring place with our formal education. Most of us won't pursue another degree and another degree for as long as we live. And we don't feel guilty about that; we're happy to have reached the level of academic growth that seems appropriate for our situation.

Can you imagine going into your thirties, forties, or fifties and stressing because you just can't seem to grow one inch taller? Once you stopped growing taller, hopefully your focus for growth became maturing: being all you can be and all you were created to be, finding your niche, and living out the life that God called you to. We recognize that this is the smart approach to growth in our personal lives—so why do we feel guilty or bad about our church maintaining a number that is within our gift mix, strengths, and calling?

Pastors, we need to recognize when we are a full-grown, God-honoring church, and stop feeling like a second-rate citizen in God's kingdom. The church is the church. House church or mega church, we all belong to God and we all have our place in His kingdom.

Have you ever felt sorry for Jesus because His church hit a plateau at twelve? Twelve was His number. Twelve was Jesus's God-honoring potential. He and His twelve disciples were small in number, but very fruitful in ministry. They made a difference right where they were, and making a difference—not numbers—is what the church should be focused on. We should focus on planting and watering in our community and around the world, and let God give the increase.

God's DNA: The Miniature Poodle and the Great Dane

This example may illustrate what nature has to teach us about normal growth. In a healthy environment, a Miniature Poodle will reach its natural size and so will a Great Dane, but they will be many pounds and inches apart. They each grow according to their DNA. A person who purchased a Great Dane puppy would be terribly disappointed if it grew to the size of a Miniature Poodle and stopped there. And no one who buys a Miniature Poodle expects it to grow to Great Dane stature—wouldn't it be a shocker if it did! Thankfully, each dog will grow to the size encoded in its own DNA. And, unlike the small church, I've never seen a Miniature Poodle stress or feel less of a dog because it couldn't reach Great Dane proportions.

So pastors and leaders, why are you so disappointed with the size of your church when you have created the healthiest possible environment for your leadership and church to reach the size encoded in their DNA? I think it is because we have been taught that all churches should become Great Danes! That we should all become big dogs, because big dogs are, well, bigger!

But are big dogs *better*? The Great Dane and the Miniature Poodle both give love and affection, and each needs attention, love, and affection from its master. Both breeds bring glory to God, their creator, by simply being who God created them to be—dogs. Our church culture as a whole has put so much emphasis on numerical growth that we have lost sight of the importance of simply being who God created us to be. If we are discouraged or disappointed from lack of numbers, that comes out of our own thoughts, not God's.

If Redwood Trees Thought Like Pastors

I read this article which got me to thinking: what if trees thought about growth in the same light as the church does?

The Coast Redwood, Tallest Tree in the World

The coast redwood (Sequoia sempervirens) towers over all other trees in the world. At 112.1 meters (367.8 feet) the coast redwood discovered on the banks of Redwood Creek by the National Geographic Society in 1963 was the tallest known tree, known as the Stratosphere Giant. However, in 2006 the world's reigning tallest living tree, seems to have lost its title to not one but three contenders.

Like the 370-foot Giant, the three trees are coast redwoods. They were discovered this summer in Redwood National Park near Eureka by a team of California researchers who spend most of their free time bushwhacking through North Coast forests in search of taller and taller trees.

So far, the group has found about 135 redwoods that reach higher than 350 feet, said team member Chris Atkins, the man credited with finding the Stratosphere Giant in August 2000 in nearby Humboldt Redwoods State Park. The tallest of the three new finds, a redwood named Hyperion, measures 378.1 feet. Next in line, Helios, stands at 376.3 feet; Icarus, the third, reaches 371.2 feet.[ii]

What if redwood trees were like our churches today? If the redwoods had bishops and conducted tree growth workshops, it might sound something like this: "The majority of our trees are under 370 feet tall, and in order to combat this shortfall we are bringing in our new tallest trees, Hyperion, Helios, and Icarus, who will be speaking on how to break the 370-foot barrier." And now, all of the trees under 370 feet who used to believe they had reached their God-honoring potential start to feel that there are greater heights that they should be reaching for. They no longer focus on producing oxygen or housing eagles and other creatures, but now much of their time is spent searching for ways to make up for the this shortfall and break the 370-foot barrier. Now their minds are filled with, "How did Hyperion, Helios, and Icarus do it? If I could purchase one of their tree growth strategy manuals, maybe I could break the 370-foot barrier."

Now, I know that is silly; trees don't feel like that—but many of our churches do! They feel that they somehow honor God less because they don't have as many members as some of the churches in their denomination or as the church down the street. But have you ever thought less of Jesus because He only had twelve in His church? You may call what Jesus did mentoring or shepherding, but the twelve disciples were His group, like your congregation is your group. Jesus invested in His twelve and you invest in your flock. It's all ministry.

It's Not Height that Brings God Glory

The redwoods reach heights of over 370 feet, while the hollies in my flower garden are only a few feet tall. God created both, so which one brings God the most glory? Which one is better? Which one serves a greater purpose? As far as which one brings God the most glory, it stands to reason that it would be the one that grew where God planted it and became what God created it to be. As far as which one is better, it would depend on what they were needed for. If you were looking for a tree to cut into lumber and build a house with, then the redwood would probably be the better choice. However, if you wanted something to plant in your front yard to beautify your landscaping, your better choice might be a holly. If you were to plant one of the giant redwoods in the front yard, it wouldn't be long until your house would look like the landscaping for the redwood! The roots could suck all of the moisture out of your soil, burst your plumbing lines, and lift your house out of the ground. The redwoods look beautiful if they are growing in the right place, and so does the church that is growing where God planted it.

I was invited to speak in Portland, Oregon, so my wife and I went up a day early, rented a car and drove up to the coast. It was the end of October and the trees were turning colors. It was a magnificent display: vibrant reds and yellows and shades of color I couldn't begin to describe. As we drove out to the coast admiring the colors, we never once focused on the size of the trees. What we did focus on was the beauty of each tree. The trees were all different in size, but what caught our eyes that day was the *beauty* of each tree, each being what God called it to be and doing what God called it to do. As each tree lived out its days and seasons it produced and projected the beauty God had placed within it. As we drove along one of us would say, "Look at that one!" Down the road a little ways and again, "Whoa, look how beautiful that one is!" The beauty came about by each tree growing where God planted it, being the tree God called it to be.

I have had the privilege of visiting many churches in different cities and states, and even in other countries, and in each one of them God showed me something beautiful. The way they worship their creator. The compelling message being preached. The richness of a Bible study lesson taught. The sacrificial givers who are meeting a need that God has laid on their hearts. The faithful Bible teachers who are investing their lives and time into children, teens, and adults, making disciples one lesson at a time. People volunteering their time and using their talents: ushering, greeting, mowing the lawn, keeping the flower gardens, cleaning the toilets, preparing meals, praising, playing their instruments, operating the sound system, running the computers, watching the babies in the nursery, leading their departments, organizing events and outreach, cleaning and filling the baptistery, performing baptisms, sending follow-up guest cards and absentee cards, taking offerings, keeping the church books, interceding, giving, and meeting needs locally, nationally, and internationally. All of these and more are a beautiful part of God's church.

And as each person of each church offers their time and talent in their respective area I truly believe God sees the beauty of each person, in the same way we see the vibrant beauty of each tree, as they are doing what God called them to do and being what God called them to be. And I don't believe that God is concerned about whether you are doing your part in a mega church or a house church, as long as you are doing and being what God called you to do and be. Jesus never mentioned the size of the church the day He saw the beauty of what God was doing through a widow who place two coins (worth about two of our pennies) in the offering. He just marveled at her sacrificial giving. I think He is still in awe of all of the folks who give sacrificially each week to their Creator.

Where Has the Feeling of Significance Gone?

Only 1 percent of churches are mega churches, which tells us that only 1 percent of pastors have been given the gifts it takes to pastor a mega church. As they use their gifts to grow their congregations, God is proud of them—but no more proud of them than He is of you and me. When we lose sight of the significance *our* churches have, we feel like failures—and that is precisely where Satan wants us. And that is where I was for a while, but no more.

As a pastor of a small church, I'm writing this book out of my past frustrations, frustrations that led to questions such as "Why can't we grow?" and "What are we doing wrong?" More than once I asked myself, "Do I need to step aside and let someone else come in and grow our church?" And I've talked to too many pastors who share similar feelings. But the truth of the matter is, God called me to pastor our church and God called you to pastor your church. And most of us invest our lives into our churches the best way we know how. We produce fruit at the pace and quantity God gave us the ability to produce, and I truly believe God has been pleased and is still pleased with that. You and I both know that everything we have done and will do will not be perfect, but God gave us a calling and a church and enough talent to produce accordingly.

Listen very carefully to what I'm about to tell you: most of the doubts I had concerning numerical growth originated from *me,* the Senior Pastor, as I would set numbers that God never ordained us to reach. And I believe most of the pastors who are now stressing over breaking the next barrier are doing so because of a church culture which we have created, based off the 1 percent of churches who have reached "mega" status. In reality, ninety-four percent of churches grow to less than 500 and 70 percent grow to less than 150. And I believe that each church will level off at a healthy number for the leadership of that church.

You can call it a plateau if you want to—I did for over twenty years—but I now truly believe that the majority of the churches have not reached a plateau, but their God-honoring potential. If the pastor and leaders are healthy, I believe each church will reach its God-ordained size according to the gifts and abilities God has given it.

No Church Keeps Growing Forever

Even pastors of medium to large churches worry about reaching what they may call a plateau. Here's an article from *Leadership Journal*, a Christian magazine, written by a pastor who took a church of eighty to ninety people in 1990 and grew it to fifteen hundred in fifteen years. Then something happened: they stopped growing numerically. Here's a part of what the pastor has to say in his article:

These years were fun, stressful, hectic, and exciting. I will never forget them!

As attendance climbed, we did the normal American thing—we built bigger facilities. We assumed the growth would never stop.

In 1996 we moved to a 14-acre campus, then in February of 2005, we moved into an even larger third campus. We beefed up our staff for the next anticipated growth phase . . .which we all knew was right around the corner.

But then something happened. We stopped accumulating numbers as we had for the previous 15 years. For the first time, we "leveled out" numerically. We kept attracting new people, but we also started losing more than we had before.

The new facility was so spacious that many were caught off guard by a feeling of "being lost in a crowd." Gradually a number of the core families, who had been a part of Midland Free for years, began making their way to the exits.

As one exiting, former elder told me, "I didn't sign up for this—large video screens and a loud band . . . no offense, but it's just not us anymore."

Over the next several years, we lost about a third of our congregation to job transfers and unhappy people leaving our church.

But something else happened, too. We backfilled the people we lost with hundreds of new folks. Today we still have about 1,500 attending, but it is a very different congregation.

We've analyzed the situation again and again and again. We've come to all sorts of conclusions about why there's so much "churn," why the total number isn't increasing. We are still attracting and retaining people, otherwise we would be one-third smaller than we are today. We are still seeing new conversions to Christ, and many getting baptized. We still hear regular stories, from the stage, about how God is touching people through the ministries of Midland Free.

Our finances are doing reasonably well, considering the economic downturn, and we are still sending people to the missions field. Our elder board is healthy, and so is our staff.

We launch new initiatives from time to time that seem to energize the congregation. Our facility is used seven days a week by those inside and outside the church, and we have numerous outreach ministries into our

*community. The consensus seems to be that the
preaching and worship services are stronger than ever .
. . but . . . we are not growing like we used to.*

*Many keep asking, "What's wrong?" I've asked it myself.
Something changed.*

*As I've thought about this situation (for five years), I've
come to the following conclusions.*[iii]

I'm want to stop here and say that I believe that
Pastor Childs represents a large group of pastors who
have great churches but who, because they aren't
perpetually increasing their numbers, feel like
something is wrong. Regardless of size, if we are not
adding significant numbers we automatically go into
the "What is wrong with us?" mode. My point is, this
mindset of numbers versus health is not just a small-
church dilemma.

And if we are not careful, we begin to entertain
the "What's wrong with us?" so much that we miss
what is so *right* with us. We stop celebrating all the
right things that are going on and become frustrated
because we can't break through to the next numerical
rung on the ladder. This is where we need to come to
a decision: "Have we reached a plateau, or have we
reached our God-honoring potential?" Pastor Childs
doesn't say in his article that his church has reached
its God-honoring potential, but he does give some

great insight to what that might look like. He describes his church as healthy.

Here's another piece of Pastor Childs's article which I think will help put church growth in right perspective:

> *Nonstop numerical growth is not a biblical expectation. Ever since eminent missiologist Donald McGavran first published his seminal thoughts on church growth, American churches have often fixated on numerical growth. The basic assumption seems to be this: all churches should be growing numerically, all the time, and something is wrong if your church isn't.*
>
> *But as I've searched the New Testament and read countless other books on the subject, this assumption seems to be alien to the Bible. There is simply no biblical expectation that a local congregation will continually grow in size, uninterrupted. That seems to be an American presupposition forced onto the Scriptures.*
>
> *If anything, Jesus told us to expect the opposite. He did promise that the gates of hell would not stand against the church, but he also commended the church in Philadelphia for standing firm though they had "little power." He never criticizes any of the seven churches in Revelation for not accumulating numbers. He does scold, however, for moral and theological compromise.*
>
> *Lesslie Newbigin writes in* The Open Secret: An Introduction to the Theology of Mission, *"Reviewing the teaching of the New Testament, one would have to say, on the one hand, there is joy in the rapid growth of the church in the earliest days, but on the other, there is not*

evidence that numerical growth of the church is a matter of primary concern. There is no shred of evidence in Paul's letters to suggest that he judged the churches by the measure of their success in rapid numerical growth. [Nowhere is there] anxiety or enthusiasm about the numerical growth of the church."

If churches never stopped growing—ever—they would take over whole towns. Why is it that virtually every church plateaus at certain sizes and stages?

The reason is that neverending growth isn't realistic; sociologically, theologically, or biblically. I was recently in Israel standing among the ruins of ancient synagogues in Capernaum, Korazin and En-Gedi. As I reflected on these ancient worship sites, I highly doubt if the leadership council at any of these synagogues ever sat around wondering why they hadn't grown recently. I doubt if they worked on gimmicks to grow as we often do in western congregations. Maybe, but I doubt it. They were people of the Book, by the Book, and for the Book—so help them God. . . . Yes, poor leaders do contribute to the decline of good churches at times. Absolutely! And sinful leaders sometimes bring a church down through stupid blunders. But sometimes they do not. Again, we are responsible for the depth, health, and outreach—God is responsible for size and scope of influence. As one wise church leader told me, "Your take care of the depth of your ministry; let God take care of the breadth."

This article revealed to me that small churches are not the only ones who struggle with lack of numbers. Every church, big or small, has a God-honoring potential, and we should stop trying so hard to grow it beyond that point.

How Do You Know if You've Reached Your God-Honoring Potential?

What we learn from nature is that a healthy animal or tree raised in a healthy environment will grow to its mature size and then stop growing. We can expect the same to be true of churches. Pastors can be confident that they have reached their God-honoring potential when they are healthy, their church is healthy, and the numbers level off. I say "level off" because we all win some and lose some for a variety of reasons.

I believe that some pastors try to take their churches beyond their God-honoring potential and suffer for it. They are like Moses, who was busy from early in the morning until late at night; that wasn't healthy for him *or* the people he was ministering to.

Reaching your God-honoring potential is about having a healthy lifestyle as a pastor, where God and family come before the church. When you try to build beyond your God-honoring potential you no longer have a church, but the church has you. I'm talking about being consumed by the church you pastor: the church is growing while your family and your personal life suffer. The truth is, even a small church can consume the pastor, especially when the pastor is trying to play "Super Pastor"! When you try to sustain a pace beyond your God-honoring potential, you will eventually experience burnout. How many disciples did God call you to pastor? Jesus's God-honoring number was twelve; what is yours?

When your church has reached its God-honoring potential, new members replace old members rather than increasing overall attendance. Our church has run around the same size for most of our twenty-five years, but we have lost many members to death or moving out of the area. Like most churches, we have people leave our church to join other churches and we inherit people who have left their churches to come to ours. That seems to be a part of the cycle of church.

It's wonderful to get new members, but we shouldn't start to expect our church to keep growing indefinitely. It will grow only until it fulfills its God-honoring potential. Going back one more time to the Miniature Poodle and the Great Dane, you can feed them the same brand of dog chow and run them through the same exercise program from birth to maturity, but the Poodle will not reach the height or size of the Dane. And pastor, you can read all the mega church materials you can get your hands on, purchase all of the mega church growth materials, and implement them the best you know how in your church, but unless God has put it into your DNA to build a mega church, you will not reach mega church status.

I Killed My Ego

I will give you a warning: if, like me, you have thought for years that you would double or quadruple your membership and it hasn't happened after your best efforts—then you may have a hard time accepting that the current size of your church is your God-honoring potential. I want to challenge you to take some time and ask yourself, "What if this is the size God has ordained our church to be?" If you can come to terms with that, you will experience such freedom. If you know that you have given your best and the current size of your church is pretty close to the size it has been for quite some time, it is likely that you have reached your God-honoring potential. If that is the case, then I would like you to repeat this statement: "Our church has not reached a plateau, but it has in fact reached its God-honoring potential!" Now, if you listen very carefully you will hear God say, "You are My beloved pastor, in whom I am well pleased!"

The church I pastor—which I pioneered—reached its current size within three years, and we have stayed around this size for twenty-five years.

While our church has been pretty consistent in our numbers for the past twenty-five years, the core members and leaders have changed about four times. People come and people go, but our church continues to make disciples, baptize, break bread, and fellowship. We are an Acts-two, God-ordained, fruit-producing, mission-giving, outreaching, people-loving, caring, fellowshipping, disciple-making, bread-breaking, praying church, and we are excited about serving the Lord! And if you accept who you are and what God ordained you to be, I bet the same could be said about you and your church.

Now, if you are a brand-new church, less than a few years old, you may not have reached your God-honoring potential. And there may be a few of you who have been given the gifts to grow a mega church and who will keep on climbing in numbers for many years. But I truly believe the majority of us will reach our God-honoring potential—the size encoded in our DNA—at some point, and I believe that at that point we should focus on health. I believe a healthy church, of any size, will provide light and life where God directs.

Healthy Growth Requires a Healthy Environment

Whether it is a tree, a plant, an animal, or a human, everything that is normal and healthy will reach its God-honoring potential. However, there are a few factors that will prevent any one of these from reaching their potential. For example, trees and plants need soil, water, and sun. For animals and humans, proper nurturing, proper nutrition, and proper amounts of clean water can make all the difference. We've all seen the pictures of undernourished babies with bloated stomachs, who—if they do survive—may never grow to the size they would have if they had had the nutrition they needed in the first few days, months, or years of their lives. An unhealthy environment has prevented them from reaching their God-honoring potential.

So, as we strive to get our churches to their God-honoring potentials, we must be sure we provide a healthy environment. A healthy church environment includes feeding on God's word and then living that word out in our daily lives. The church is a lot like our natural bodies; if we put good stuff in and exercise, we enjoy good health.

Disease also plays a role in stunting the growth of living things. And sometimes disease or sin can strike a church (large or small), and that can hinder its growth. However, I think the time has come to acknowledge that there are many small churches that are healthy and have reached their God-honoring potential. They should by all means celebrate what God is doing in and through their church body.

Healthy Pastor Equals Healthy Church

Sometimes the church can decline because the pastor gets caught up in doing for everyone else. It's not unusual for pastors and leaders to be pulled off course, away from their gifts and strengths, to serve where some of the church leaders or members want them to serve. This is especially true for the senior pastor when too many congregants want only the senior pastor to "pray with me," "visit me," "counsel me," "baptize me," "do my wedding." None of those things are wrong, but if we are not careful even a small church can become an unhealthy church because we are so scattered. And let's not forget that God has ordained the pastor to equip saints for the work of the ministry. As pastors remain in the areas of their strengths and gifts, they remain healthy and thus will help produce a healthy church. And a healthy church will reach its God-honoring potential.

Our church experienced a great freedom when we stopped trying to be what God had called some *other* church to be and started simply being who God called *us* to be. When I stopped doing ministry in areas outside of my God-given gifts and strengths, and started developing and equipping others who were able and called to work in these areas, I—and, in turn, our church—became much healthier. For example, my strengths are developing leaders and teaching, and most of my time is spent in these two areas. Most of my leadership development is done in one-on-one sessions with our leaders and with their teams as needed.

We have such faithful leaders, but we have *developed* faithful leaders because we exalt all leaders as equals. We teach that each department leader has a pulpit, not just the preachers, teachers, and praise team. For example, the gardeners' pulpit is the flower gardens, and we ask them, "What kind of message do people see as they drive into the church parking lots and look at your garden?" For the cooks we ask, "What kind of sermon are you cooking up today?" The one they really get a kick out of is, "Don't burn your sermon!"

I believe that a healthy church is one in which we give individuals opportunity to do the ministry they are called to do and treat them as equals as we serve our communities and the world around us.

Learning to Appreciate the Size of Your Church

The majority of churches in the United States are small churches. According to Gary McIntosh in the book *One Size Doesn't Fit All*:

> *75 percent of all churches have fewer than 149 worshippers on a Sunday morning. ... Most churches are fairly small with 50 percent of all churches under 100, and 80 percent under 200 in average attendance on an average Sunday morning. ... The remaining 20 percent of all churches are evenly divided between medium and large churches. According to the best estimates, 10 percent of churches are between 200 and 400 in size, with the remaining 10 percent more than 400. ...Less than 1 percent of all churches fall into the category of a mega church, having 2,000 or more worshipers.[iv]*

This chart, excerpted from McIntosh's book, shows those statistics in more detail:

Attendance Percentile:[v]

2000+	*99%*
800-1999	*98%*
400-799	*95%*

250-399	90%
200-249	85%
150-199	80%
140-149	75%
130-139	70%
100-129	60%
75-99	50%
55-74	40%
45-54	35%
40-44	30%
35-39	25%
30-34	20%
25-29	15%
20-24	10%
19 or less	5%

What do you see when you look at those numbers? I used to see how small our numbers looked compared to the top 2 percent, but now I see the body of Christ and I feel so blessed that we make up a part of that number. To be called and chosen to pastor a part of Christ's body is awesome! And wherever your church is on the scale, we need each other and we are all here to complete each other, not to compete with each other. All that God requires is for you, as a pastor, be a good steward over what He has given you.

Most small-church pastors and leaders that I know and respect are neither lazy nor incompetent. In fact, most of the pastors I know are very good stewards over their churches. They pursue some sort of personal growth—whether through seminars, books, or leadership events—with some consistency, as best they can while attending to their other pastoral duties such as counseling, conducting weddings and funerals, preparing two or three sermons or Bible study lessons a week, teaching a new believers' class, putting out fires, recruiting help for vacant ministry, and overseeing the budget—and many do this as they work a full-time or part-time job outside the church! If you are acting as a good steward to your church, and creating a healthy environment for it to grow, then you shouldn't feel like a failure just because you're not in the top 2 percent in size. Instead, you should feel confident that your church is exactly the size God ordained it to be, just as the Miniature Poodle is exactly the size God encoded into its DNA.

Churches of All Sizes Are Part of God' s Plan

I thank God for *all* churches of *all* sizes. We each make up the body of Christ, and His DNA runs through each church that has made Him Lord. And we each play a very important role, especially within each of our own communities. Each church, regardless of size, has a mandate from heaven to reach out and make a difference. And God has planted all kinds of diverse churches across the globe, according to the specific needs of each city or community. Each church brings life and light to its tiny part of this vast world. And it is high time that we recognize that each church—which includes *your* church—is God's hands extended. We should celebrate what God is allowing each of us to contribute.

Here's a good example of a small church celebrating what God is doing in their midst. I spoke on the purpose and power of the average church to a group of pastors and leaders in Atlanta, and this is what Dr. Driver, the host pastor, had to say about their church: "We are a small church doing mega ministry!" Don't you just love that? That's the way I feel about every church that teaches and preaches

Jesus Christ and reaches outside its own walls to bless others. *That* is ministry, whether the congregation is twenty or twenty thousand.

Dr. Driver's church has a food pantry and a clothing ministry; they teach, train, and equip, locally and internationally. And I am quite sure that each person who is receiving food, clothing, teaching, and training from Dr. Driver's church finds that the church is making a mega difference in their personal lives. The same can be said for each person who is being fed, clothed, and ministered to by *your* church.

As a pastor of a small church for more than twenty-five years who has spent the last several years wrestling with questions concerning church growth, allow me to share some of the thoughts that have helped me see the small church the way I believe God intends for it to be seen.

I have just moved to a small town which is large enough to have a Walmart, and this Walmart store has a pretty good selection of meat, including steaks. I thoroughly enjoy a good steak, but when I go shopping for a steak, I don't go to Walmart. Guess why? It's because we have two little meat markets that offer fresh steaks that are to die for. Both of them are in old, plain buildings, and both of them do a great business. Simply put, they feed the need for a great steak for many people, including me. These little meat markets don't have a nice supercenter building, they don't offer anywhere near the variety of produce Walmart offers, and they don't serve the masses that Walmart serves, but they serve a good many of us who are grateful for their service.

And there are a great number of people who have these same sorts of feelings about their small church. Their church doesn't have a new mega building, or serve the masses, but what their church serves feeds them like no other place in town. If we minister to their needs, they don't care about the size of the church.

Jesus made it very clear that significant, God-honoring ministry is not about numbers, but about personal ministry. Matthew 25:40: "And the King will answer and say to them, 'Assuredly, I say to you, inasmuch as you did it to one of the least of these My brethren, you did it to Me.'"

Transformation is what people are looking for. When I was fifteen I gave my heart to Jesus and was forever changed in a little country church, Dolberg Missionary Baptist Church, where maybe thirty others were gathered. That was more than forty years ago and that little church is still there. Some of the same saints who were doing ministry when I found Jesus are still there, being light and salt to a little rural part of Oklahoma. One little birthing station God placed there decades ago, still shining its light. The pastor and I both preached my mother's funeral there last year. It had been Mother's home church since she was a little girl. This small church is still a great birthing place and is responsible for producing many pastors and Christ followers in its part of the Oklahoma. God has placed churches just like this all over the world, and they are the most powerful points of light on the planet.

To the pastors and leaders who are parents, let me ask you something. If one of your kids turned eighteen and moved a thousand miles away and joined a church that loved them and taught them God's Word and gave them a place to use their gifts and talents, would that church be a huge blessing to you as a dad or mom? Of course it would. Why? Because that church is being a blessing to your kid. You wouldn't be concerned about the size of the church; what is important is its investment in your kid. Well, guess what? Each person who comes to my church or your church is one of God's children, and He is thrilled with our investment in His kids. Investing in people is what the church is called to do, regardless of its size.

Don't Apologize for Your Size

We have created a church culture where it is hard to appreciate the significance of small churches and all they do. It is as though a church of fifty being light and salt is somehow less God-honoring than a church of ten thousand.

Of all the people on the planet, we should be *most* excited about what we are providing for our communities. We are the keepers of the Holy Bible! As we preach it and teach it, individuals and families are transformed from darkness into His marvelous light. We are keepers of God's truth, entrusted to share it with whomever God brings into our path.

My church and your church, regardless of size, will meet certain needs in our own respective communities, and yet we feel like second-class pastors and leaders because we can't increase our numbers on Sunday. We act as though the good that God has called us to do and that we are doing is not enough, simply because we can't grow a larger attendance. And I think that breaks God's heart. When my kids and grandkids use the talents and abilities that God gave them, when they are who God called them to be, I am so proud of them! And from what I can gather from God's Word, that's how God feels about us whenever we use the gifts and talents He blessed us with.

What I have observed about some small churches is that they are more aware of what they are *not* than what they *are*. What about you? If someone asks you to tell them about your church and what God has called you to do, what do you tell them? Is it positive? Are you excited about what your church is doing? Why or why not?

I'm a nationally certified life coach, and some of the pastors I have had the privilege of coaching would begin to tell me about their churches by saying things like, "We are a small church; we don't have … we can't … we're not …" etc. All the good they are doing seems to be over shadowed by what they are not. God doesn't call us to be all things to all men; not even a mega church can pull that off. However, He *has* called each church to minister to specific people and specific needs.

Something that has been such a blessing to our church is that we celebrate what God is doing in and through us instead of giving attention to what we are not. We acknowledge that God has enabled us to make a significant difference in the lives of others and we know that God rejoices over that, so we do too. The people whose lives God has allowed us to touch and change look at our church and see God's love and light. And the same can be said for your church and all that you do for God's glory.

Learning to Appreciate the Talents God has Given You

In Matthew 25, the parable of the talents, the master gives five, two, and one talents to three different servants, according to each one's own ability, for them to use for his purpose. Similarly, God has given you and me different gifts and talents in different amounts, according to our own ability, for His purpose. If God gave you the gifts and talent to build a mega church and you didn't, then you wouldn't be in good standing with Him. We need to remember that the only one in this parable who is reprimanded by his master is the one who hides his talent. The one who hides his talent also has a distorted picture of who his master really is. He perceives the master to be a hard man, reaping where he has not sown, and he tells his master this as he is handing his seed back to him. Next, the man uses the excuse that he was afraid and that's why he didn't invest what the master had given him. The master speaks the truth and says that it wasn't fear that kept this man from sowing the talent he had been given; the truth of the matter was that the servant was wicked and lazy. And just like this man, when we live in sin and laziness we develop a distorted view of our Heavenly Father, which will cause us to pull away from God and lose our God-given ability to produce fruit.

If you were to ask the servant who was given five talents and the one who was given two talents what they thought of their master, both would paint a picture of a generous, loving master. I believe the same can be said for both mega church pastors and small church pastors. When we simply utilize all the talents God has given us, He is pleased and we are blessed. And whether you pastor a mega church or house church, all that is required is to use the talent God gave you. Everyone's talents are needed, because all churches of all sizes make up the body of Christ. The faithful mega church pastors will receive their reward according to how they used what God gave them, and it will be the same for the faithful pastors of small churches. For the majority of us who do not pastor a mega church, if we are faithful over our flocks then we will also hear our Master say, "Well done, good and faithful servant!"

Mega Church = Mega Obstacles

The mega church deals with some of the same issues that the smaller church deals with, but usually in mega proportions. I heard one mega church pastor declare that this was the last sanctuary that he would ever build. So, what will his church do? If they keep adding hundreds each year, they will have to add more and more worship services to accommodate the crowds.

Mega churches are a fairly new phenomenon and it will be interesting to see how they will handle growth if one congregation reaches 100,000, 200,000 or 300,000. Some are starting satellite churches located in different parts of their city or state, and some even have satellite churches in other states. Major increases in numbers will eventually create the need for major changes.

Dealing with these problems takes a person to whom God has given the ability to handle mega problems. I heard a mega church pastor at a leadership conference say his church had an $18 million shortfall for a building project it was engaged in. He and his church overcame that $18 million shortfall and finished its building. As a small church pastor, that blows my mind! They overcame the shortfall because God gave this leader the ability to rally the troops and make up the $18 million.

Your church has its own set of needs and creates its own set of messes, and God gave you— pastor and leaders—the ability to deal with the needs, the numbers, and the messes your size church can create. And providing ministry to ten who have needs and problems is just as significant to the ten as providing ministry to ten thousand who also have needs and problems. We *should* believe that, but as pastors of small churches we seem to have lost sight of that reality.

The Stresses of Pastoring a Larger Church

I've heard testimonies of pastors who face burnout or who have a family crisis and divorce, because at some point they didn't have a church, but the church had them. Working seven days a week, putting in fifteen-hour days, is not a sustainable pace for anyone. The same can be said for pastors of smaller churches, who seem to think they have to do the majority of the ministry: teaching, preaching, counseling, performing weddings and funerals, chairing every meeting, and being involved with every special event. They can experience burnout as well, if they don't utilize their church members' gifts.

Maybe you're in the 94 percent who have fewer than 500 and you've thought for quite some time that you have the ability to pastor a church of at least a thousand. Well, here's what the church experts say it will take to manage a church of one thousand: "Some of the problems the pastor will face when he gets to 1,000:

- *Increased number of personal problems among individuals.*

- *Increased number of paid ministers to manage.*

- *Increased number of paid staff to supervise.*

- *Building a cohesive vision to an enlarged following.*

- *Developing harmony among paid ministers and staff.*

- *Lack of parking.*

- *Inadequate size of the building.*

- *Logistical problems, that is, moving a larger number of people in and out of limited space in a short period of time.*

- *Need for increased finances to pay for expansion.*

- *Need for expert money management.*

- *Need for personnel administration.*

- *Increased audio/sound problems.*

- *Worshipers are detached from platform in large auditoriums.*

- *Impersonalization among worshipers and between members grows.*

- *Senior pastor's inability to manage growing numbers of paid ministers and staff.*

- *Senior pastor's inability to delegate ministry through staff.*

- *Need for new forms of advertising to reach the masses.*

- *Unreached number of prospects in community dries up.*

- *The sin of an 'Achan' is more likely to occur in a large ministerial or paid staff that will siphon off growth momentum and/or harmony.*

- *Burnout in senior pastor.*

- *As facilities grow older, institutional blight develops in building, organization, and/or vision."[vi]*

Just reading that is stressful for me, and it makes me appreciate the church I pastor. However, that wouldn't be draining to the pastor who has been given the gift to build a church of a thousand, and whose church is that large; he would just look at those statements, chuckle, and say, "Yeah, that's sounds about right!"

Even after reading the long list of added stresses the church pastor of a thousand must endure, there are still some small church pastors who feel they could handle all of that, if they could just reach a thousand. The truth is, if you could handle all of that, you would be able to build a church of a thousand. That's what you have to settle in your heart and mind, pastor. If God gives you the talent to build a church of thousands you can, but if He hasn't given you that gift, use what you have and build it to the place God gave you talent to reach. And that is reaching your God-honoring potential.

To the pastor who has a family and who is spending long hours away from your family building the church, answer this question: what do your spouse and children truly think about the church? Do they light up with joy when they talk about it, or do they see the church as something that consumes you and takes you away from them? It has been my experience as I have had the opportunity to speak to pastors in the United States and other countries that this is a problem. There are too many pastors working way too many hours a week, which is causing all kinds of health problems for the pastors and all kinds of family problems. I recently heard a bishop address this subject; he said he was tired of doing the funerals of pastors who were way too young and shouldn't have been dying. He gave a great message on living a balanced life and learning how to delegate.

No One's Exempt from Church Envy

A mega church is a church of two thousand or more, but the largest church in the U.S.—Lakewood Church in Houston, Texas—has more than 43,500 in weekly attendance.[vii] Its pastor, Joel Osteen, had to purchase Compaq Center to fit them all! I'm not sure if even 1 percent of the ministers who pastor mega churches have the gifts to develop and pastor a church the size of Joel Osteen's. And with the church culture we have created, I wonder how the mega church pastor deals with the fact that Pastor Osteen's church is so much larger than theirs. Do they have those same conversations, asking themselves, "Why can't we grow to forty-three thousand; why are we stuck at ten thousand?"

And even the biggest American mega church would be considered a small church in comparison to Yoido Full Gospel Church, an Assemblies of God congregation in Seoul, South Korea. Yoido Full Gospel is the world's largest church, with around a million members. According to an article in *The Economist,* "If you want to attend one of the two services starring the church's founder, David Yonggi Cho, you need to be an hour early or you won't get in."[viii] Pastor Cho could do workshops no other mega church pastor could: "How to Grow Your Church to One Million." His church makes the mega churches in the USA look like house churches. However, we don't think in those terms—and neither should we think in those terms when it comes to how large God wants to grow our church. Church is church.

I receive a leadership tape each month from a well-known leadership guru, and I love to listen to him. In his latest CD he spoke of a young pastor who had eighteen thousand in Sunday attendance, and he proudly boasted that this young man has more people in his restroom on Sunday than most pastors have in their church. That's probably a true statement, but I'm not sure how significant it is. I guess it was said to honor this pastor, but it's not very edifying to the majority of the body. He could have said, "There were more people in the restroom of this pastor's church than there were in Jesus's twelve-man church," but my thought is, so what? Pastor Cho could probably make the same statement: "We have more people in our restrooms on Sunday than the mega churches in America have in their entire church!" My point is, as Christ-followers it is nor our place to make condemning statements about other churches, regardless of size.

A Snapshot of the Small Church

One of the powerful things about the small church is that we are able to build authentic relationships. Our smaller numbers affords us the opportunity to invest our time in making disciples. We celebrate each other; we attend each other's weddings and funerals and model how to live life and how to deal with death when we lose a loved one or friend. There are some who refer to small churches as social clubs, but I believe that Jesus modeled the importance of building close relationships and community. Any size church can become a social club, but I don't believe that is the intent of most churches.

Jesus knew His twelve in a very intimate way, and most small churches that I am familiar with enjoy that same kind of intimacy. They enjoy familiar faces and being able to know most of the people they worship with. They like the small-church-family atmosphere their church provides. It's a good fit for them. And many small churches have families who raised their kids, grandkids, and great grandkids in them; these kinds of churches have been the spiritual bedrock for these families for generations.

Paul sent greetings to the house churches in Romans 16:5, Colossians 4:15, and Philemon 1:2—and never once did he add a "P.S. You should have already outgrown your house by now" or "I'm praying that you'll break fifty by this time next year" or "Your annual church report indicates that you haven't won one soul all year; come on, you should be able to stumble across one soul!"

Listen, over the past twenty-five years our church has consistently: won the lost, baptized new believers, invested in making disciples, developed many leaders, and given countless opportunities for people to discover and use their gifts and talents.

These individuals may not have been able to use their gifts and talents in a mega church, simply because of the level of talent the mega church has available to it, but they definitely were and are a blessing to our church. As these individuals use their gifts and talents and we each give out of who we are, our church has become a blessing to our community and other parts of the world. To the best of our ability, we are utilizing what God has given us.

Your church is a light in a dark corner of the world, placed precisely where God placed you to shine. So, with all the resources and talent you have, shine! With all the love you can give away, shine! With all the kindness God can pour in you and through you, shine! Find the niche in your part of the world that God has ordained you to fill. Ask God to help your light to shine in your community. Ask for influence in your neighborhood. Help out where you can and God will present an opportunity for you to share His love and light with someone.

One of my friends, who is an overseer in his denomination, shared that in his denomination most of the money for missions and operations comes from healthy churches that run around 150 to 250. Churches that are healthy can make a significant difference, regardless of size. Think about this: if all of the churches who have 499 or fewer in attendance shut down today, that means that 94 percent of the churches would close. Think of the serious impact that would have on our planet.

Clarify Your Mission

> *Jesus said to him, "'You shall love the Lord your God with all your heart, with all your soul, and with all your mind.' This is the first and great commandment. And the second is like it: 'You shall love your neighbor as yourself.' On these two commandments hang all the Law and the Prophets."*
>
> *—Matthew 22:37-39[ix]*

The first and great commandment is to love God. We love God by spending time with Him and sharing a personal, intimate relationship with Him, much like we do with the people we love. The second commandment Jesus gave was to love our neighbor—not to win our neighbor. Sometimes it feels like we have replaced *loving* our neighbor with strategies and methods for *winning* our neighbor. Jesus's life is a model of loving God and loving people. Those two things were a part of His daily agenda. I know the great commission of making disciples is important, but it is the process of truly loving our neighbor and building a relationship with them that increases our chances of sharing the love and light of Jesus with them someday.

For the small church, we don't have the financial resources to hire professionals to carry out the calling of the church, but we do have the unlimited resource of God's love. I am convinced that if we follow these two commandments and focus on loving God first and loving our neighbors, which to me is the great commission, God will grow our churches to their God-honoring potential.

Jesus's Church

Jesus chose twelve. He could have had a mega church, but He didn't; He had twelve. One might argue that Jesus didn't have a church, but He did shepherd the twelve, and they did operate as an Acts two church. He taught them doctrine, and He and His disciples practiced fellowship, breaking of bread, and praying together. Jesus's church was about the size of most house churches or cell groups. Jesus had a few folks whom He had healed offer to follow Him, but He turned them down. He did invite the rich man in Matthew 19 to sell his riches and follow Him, but the rich man refused Jesus's invitation. The point is that Jesus's God-honoring potential for His church was twelve.

Small in Number, Clear in Mission

Jesus's church was small in number, but He was very clear in what God had called Him to do. Here is Jesus's mission statement: "the Son of Man has come to seek and to save that which was lost" (Luke 19:10). Or as Luke 4:18-21 puts it:

"The Spirit of the Lord is upon Me,

Because He has anointed Me

To preach the gospel to the poor;

He has sent Me to heal the brokenhearted,

To proclaim liberty to the captives

And recovery of sight to the blind,

To set at liberty those who are oppressed;

To proclaim the acceptable year of the Lord."

Not only did Jesus know clearly what His mission was, He also knew who He was sent to minister to: Israelites. When the woman in Matthew 15 came to Jesus and begged Him to cast the demon out of her daughter, Jesus hesitated. Why? Jesus gave the answer in verse 24: "I was not sent except to the lost sheep of the house of Israel." Jesus wasn't being hard or callous, but he was very focused on fulfilling God's purpose. That's all God requires.

It is not the size of your church that matters. What is vitally important is: what has God called you and your church to do, and whom has He called you to invest in? There are so many needs in the world and each church has a limited number of resources, so it is important that we each diligently seek God's direction for where the majority of our time, talent, and resources should be invested.

We learn from Jesus that, when we invest our time and resources in the people and places He has called us to, He will provide in supernatural ways. In Matthew 14, for example, Jesus ministered to the multitude and God took five loaves and two fish and fed five thousand men and all the women and children. In the church I pastor, we have learned to be very careful about where we give. We have our intercessors petition God at the beginning of each year asking for God's divine direction on where we are to give. As a result, our church has been able to increase our giving and our general operations account has more than doubled.

Making Disciples is Hard Work

In order to make mature disciples we have to focus a good amount of our time on developing them. It's not the size of your church that matters most, but the size of your church's disciples. The command is to make disciples, not to stress over how many you are (or are not) making. Reach out to the lost, but trust God to give the increase. Sometimes in the New Testament He added thousands to the church with one outreach message, but other times He added one or two.

Making disciples is one of the toughest things that I have experienced as a pastor. What a risk we pastors take as we invest hours and hours of our time and resources into others. And once we bring a disciple along to a place of maturity, they may bolt off to some new adventure, taking with them all of the energy, training, and time we invested. Of course, that just comes with the territory. At the end of Jesus's time on earth, all twelve of His disciples scattered. It wasn't pretty.

Then there are the disciples we invest in who become distracted and won't use their gifts, or the ones who make it to a certain level of maturity and then fall by the wayside as they are choked out with the cares of this world and its riches. When that happens, it can feel like one of your own kids falling away.

Sometimes we can beat ourselves up when it comes to making disciples, especially when we have invested so much into their lives and they seem to fall so short of their potential. Something that helped me put disciple-making in perspective was looking at some of the things Jesus encountered as He developed His disciples.

Jesus handpicked twelve disciples. And after he invested over three years of His life in teaching, modeling ministry, rebuking, loving, and providing for them, they still looked pretty rough around the edges. We will look at four of His disciples who had very distinct personality traits. These same personality traits still exist in the church today, and for those of you who oversee employees in the business world, these personality traits are there as well.

The Strong-Willed Influencer

First, let's look at Peter. Peter's motto is, "Ready, Fire, Aim!" Peter is a bottom-line, big-picture, in-your-face, influential leader. And, true to form, here's Pete:

> *From that time Jesus began to show to His disciples that*
> *He must go to Jerusalem, and suffer many things from*
> *the elders and chief priests and scribes, and be killed,*
> *and be raised again the third day.*

> Then Peter took Him aside and began to rebuke Him, saying, "Far be it from You, Lord; this shall not happen to You!"
>
> But He turned and said to Peter, "Get behind Me, Satan! You are an offense to Me, for you are not mindful of the things of God, but the things of men. (Matthew 16:21-23).

Influential, strong leaders like Peter are able to sway the general thoughts in any given room, and evidently that is what Pete is attempting to do on this particular occasion. Jesus has to come back with a really strong rebuke—the kind of rebuke that could send the average person into deep shock, so that they wind up in the fetal position sucking their thumb. But this is the type of language strong-willed, influential leaders understand. And when you have someone like Pete who is really opposed to your vision, things can go south very quickly unless you address it promptly and strongly. Once Jesus is through bringing Peter back to reality, He turns to His disciples and gives them the "it's time to take up your cross and die to self" speech.

And I don't know about you, but I would have been plenty nervous about Peter if I were in Jesus's shoes. Jesus is grooming Peter to be the keynote speaker for the first New Testament message, but just days before Pete is scheduled to preach the most important message of his life and the most important message in history, he gets all flustered because Jesus won't allow him to use the sword and protect Him from the bad guys. Remember, Pete has been rebuked for wanting to protect Jesus from this hour, but he hasn't laid it to rest yet. One thing I have learned about strong-willed people like Pete is, they may be saying yes on the outside, but not agreeing on the inside. That's why we call them "strong-willed."

Put yourself in Jesus's place: your keynote speaker, whom you have been grooming for more than three years, narrowly misses severing a person's head from his body. If Pete had been a nanosecond faster or Malchus had been a nanosecond slower, the Gospel story would have been, "And Jesus picked up Malchus's head and stuck in back on his body and healed him." That would have been pretty cool!

But wait, Pete isn't done yet. Keep imagining this from Jesus's perspective: in the midst of the anti-Christ protesters, Peter is asked if he is one of your disciples and he lies and says that he is not. When the protesters press your star disciple and insist that he has been seen hanging out with you, he begins to curse and swear and assure them that he has never even met you! That would be tough to swallow, especially if you had invested the bigger part of three years of teaching and training into his life.

If you were in Jesus's shoes witnessing what Pete had done, would you allow Pete to take the pulpit in such an important time in history and with such an important message? If you knew that some of the same people who heard Peter cursing, lying, and denying would be in the audience of that first New Testament message, would you still let him preach? That was a tough discipleship decision Jesus had to make. Well, it may not have been hard for Jesus to make it, but it would have been a tough one for most of us.

With all of his goof-ups, Pete is still in charge. When Jesus has finished His work here on earth and resurrected and met with His disciples, it seems that Pete is still not very happy about how it has all turned out. He seems to be contemplating going back to fishing for a living—and if he does, he won't be going alone:

> *Simon Peter, Thomas called the Twin, Nathanael of Cana in Galilee, the sons of Zebedee, and two others of His disciples were together. Simon Peter said to them, "I am going fishing."*
>
> *They said to him, "We are going with you also." They went out and immediately got into the boat, and that night they caught nothing (John 21:2-3).*

Jesus models how to handle an influencer: he goes out to where Pete and his followers are and engages them in conversation. He not only engages them in conversation, He engages them in *relevant* conversation—he talks about the issues His disciples are dealing with. Don't miss this, pastors and leaders. Jesus doesn't jump right to "Let's cut to the chase and get down to business; you all know why I'm here." No. He asks about their night of fishing. Jesus first connects with them and shows concern for what they are doing. Next, He listens to them, and then He speaks to their needs, which leads to a huge blessing: a net full of big fish. They catch so many fish that they are surprised that the net doesn't break. And once it dawns on them who it is that has just given them this blessed advice, they head to shore. Specifically, they head to shore following Peter, the influencer.

Once they arrive at the shore Jesus still doesn't talk about ministry, but continues ministering to their needs and cooks them up some fish for breakfast. When breakfast is ready, Jesus takes the initiative and serves them. And finally, after breakfast, Jesus gets around to the business at hand. Just in case you missed it, Jesus is teaching that relationship comes first, then ministry. "So when they had eaten breakfast, Jesus said to Simon Peter, 'Simon, son of Jonah, do you love Me more than these?' He said to Him, 'Yes, Lord; You know that I love You.' He said to him, 'Feed My lambs'" (John 21:15). I can see Jesus pointing at all of the fish in the net as He asks Pete,

"Are you going to pursue fish or My sheep?" And all eyes are on Pete, the influencer, as Jesus continues to press the issue. Jesus knows if Pete puts down the nets and goes back to preaching and teaching, so will the rest of his crew.

Every church has its influencers, and if we build healthy, loving relationships with them they will lead their followers along with them.

The "I'll Sell You Out in a Heartbeat" Disciple

Another distinct personality Jesus had to deal with is that of Judas—Judas the betrayer, the one who values money over friendship and loyalty. Here's a sample of what Jesus has to put up with from His disciple Judas Iscariot:

> A dinner was prepared in Jesus's honor. Martha served, and Lazarus sat at the table with him. Then Mary took a twelve-ounce jar of expensive perfume made from essence of nard, and she anointed Jesus's feet with it and wiped his feet with her hair. And the house was filled with fragrance.
>
> But Judas Iscariot, one of his disciples—the one who would betray him—said, "That perfume was worth a small fortune. It should have been sold and the money given to the poor." Not that he cared for the poor—he was a thief who was in charge of the disciples' funds, and he often took some for his own use. (John 12:2-6 NLT)

I'm sure Jesus knew that Judas was taking money from the funds they had, but it is very intriguing to me that Jesus never took the moneybag away from Judas. Our church discovered a Judas in our midst who was stealing church funds from one of our ministries, but we took the moneybag away from him.

As much as it hurts when we discover we have people in our church who betray us—which can be in a variety of ways, not just theft—it shouldn't come as a shock. It happened to Jesus in a small, handpicked group of twelve, and it is likely that you will have to deal with a Judas someday, if you haven't already. Even when the truth of a betrayer comes out, it can be very difficult to know exactly how to handle the situation. In the ordeal our church dealt with, the man and his wife were very involved in the church, and because of the nature of her role we had to relieve both of them of their duties. It was heartbreaking for everyone.

Jesus models how to handle a Judas. First, He identifies Judas for what he is, a betrayer. Second, He never stops calling Judas friend, leaving the door of friendship and repentance open. If we are to have hope of turning a betrayer around, we have to leave the door open as well. Treating them as a friend leaves us open and vulnerable, but it is proof of God's unconditional love working in us. And if we have a hard time calling them friend, just remember this: if they don't change their ways, they will eventually wind up hitting rock bottom, much like Judas did. When they do, we will have a sense of relief knowing that we didn't contribute to their guilt and shame by stacking on condemning words of our own.

The Doubter

The third personality type belongs to Thomas—Doubting Thomas. Thomas and those in our churches like Thomas have the ability to suck all of the faith out of a room. They have the gift of seeing why or how any plan or strategy we intend to initiate in our church is flawed and will most likely end in destruction. Here's an example of Thomas in action:

Now a certain man was sick, Lazarus of Bethany, the town of Mary and her sister Martha. It was that Mary who anointed the Lord with fragrant oil and wiped His feet with her hair, whose brother Lazarus was sick. Therefore the sisters sent to Him, saying, "Lord, behold, he whom You love is sick."

When Jesus heard that, He said, "This sickness is not unto death, but for the glory of God, that the Son of God may be glorified through it." [NOTE: Jesus clearly states God's purpose to His disciples.]

Now Jesus loved Martha and her sister and Lazarus. So, when He heard that he was sick, He stayed two more days in the place where He was. Then after this He said to the disciples, "Let us go to Judea again."

The disciples said to Him, "Rabbi, lately the Jews sought to stone You, and are You going there again?" [Which being interpreted, "Do we have to go there again?"]

Jesus answered, "Are there not twelve hours in the day? If anyone walks in the day, he does not stumble, because he sees the light of this world. But if one walks in the night, he stumbles, because the light is not in him." These things He said, and after that He said to them, "Our friend Lazarus sleeps, but I go that I may wake him up."

Then His disciples said, "Lord, if he sleeps he will get well." However, Jesus spoke of his death, but they thought that He was speaking about taking rest in sleep.

Then Jesus said to them plainly, "Lazarus is dead. And I am glad for your sakes that I was not there, that you may believe. Nevertheless let us go to him."

Then Thomas, who is called the Twin, said to his fellow disciples, "Let us also go, that we may die with Him." (John 11:1-16)

Doubters like Thomas can't seem to help themselves when it comes to speaking doubt. They appear to believe that they are the only ones who can see the risk involved and how bad things could be, and they are compelled to share their insightful thoughts out loud.

Jesus is talking about raising the dead, and all Thomas can see is death and destruction. Haven't we all been in meetings where we are excited about launching a new ministry and someone in the crowd feels strongly compelled to remind us of how a similar ministry was attempted in the spring of 1972? And they can describe each detail of the horrible aftermath it left behind, then conclude, "But you're the leaders, and if you want to put us at risk like that, it's up to you."

Jesus doesn't give a rebuke or even a mention to Thomas's statement of gloom and doom, but He does go on with God's plan. And as life-draining as a doubter's statements can be, the best thing we can do for them is to go ahead and work our plans. It's sad, but even when we have successfully completed our plans and all the fruit is on the vine, the doubter will most likely have new doubts and concerns about the next path God leads us down.

According to scripture, Thomas never grows past expressing his doubts:

> They told [Thomas], "We have seen the Lord!"
>
> But he replied, "I won't believe it unless I see the nail wounds in his hands, put my fingers into them, and place my hand into the wound in his side."
>
> Eight days later the disciples were together again, and this time Thomas was with them. The doors were locked; but suddenly, as before, Jesus was standing among

them. He said, "Peace be with you." Then he said to Thomas, "Put your finger here and see my hands. Put your hand into the wound in my side. Don't be faithless any longer. Believe!"

"My Lord and my God!" Thomas exclaimed. (John 20:25-28, NLT)

Thomas's disbelief is an aggravation to Jesus. Jesus has come to give His disciples instructions on reaching the world with a new message of hope, but before He can begin He has to clear the doubt that Thomas has dragged into the room. Thomas followed Jesus for more than three years and saw more miracles than he could count, but that doesn't stop Thomas from doubting. So we might as well know that there will be doubting disciples in our midst, and about the best we can do is tell them what Jesus told Thomas: "Don't be faithless any longer. Believe!" One other thing that I have found to be helpful: don't allow the doubters in any of your creative, vision-building meetings. Give them a simple task that doesn't require much faith. Let them cut the grass. At least when they have doubts about getting rid of all the weeds in the lawn, you can send them to Home Depot to buy some more weed killer. Just a thought.

The Ideal Disciple

God seems to balance out the hard heads, the betrayers, and the doubters with a few disciples who truly love their leaders. Jesus had one in His twelve: John the beloved. John was always in Jesus's inner circle. He loved Jesus so much that he was sure that Jesus felt that same kind of love for him; that's why he refers to himself as "the disciple whom Jesus loved." And when Jesus was going to the mountain to pray, John was in that inner circle. When Jesus sent two of His disciples ahead to reserve a room for them, he sent Peter the bold, but He also sent John, the one He knew would have His best interests at heart.

Wouldn't we all love to have a church full of people like John? We know that their hearts are for us. We can trust their motives. They don't have a hidden agenda they are trying to push. They amen our sermons, they laugh at our jokes, and they love being around us. It probably wouldn't be healthy to have an entire church board made up of these sort of people; however, Jesus modeled that it is good to have someone like John in our inner circle.

As good as it feels to have people like John in our circles, they have their issues as well. They feel that no one can preach and teach like "my pastor" can, and they don't care to hear anyone preach but you.

Now John answered Him, saying, "Teacher, we saw someone who does not follow us casting out demons in Your name, and we forbade him because he does not follow us."

But Jesus said, "Do not forbid him, for no one who works a miracle in My name can soon afterward speak evil of Me. 'For he who is not against us is on our side.'" (Mark 9:38-40)

Listen, pastor: those who have an unconditional love for you and think you can do no wrong sometimes find it difficult to allow anyone else to minister to them or minister with them. Of course, the downside to that can be that, if they have needs, they only want *you* to minister to them.

Also, John is so close to Jesus that he is quite certain Jesus will grant him almost any request he brings to Jesus. For example:

Then James and John, the sons of Zebedee, came to Him, saying, "Teacher, we want You to do for us whatever we ask."

And He said to them, "What do you want Me to do for you?"

They said to Him, "Grant us that we may sit, one on Your right hand and the other on Your left, in Your glory." (Mark 10:35-37)

Jesus has to explain to them that they really don't know what they are asking, and that it isn't His place, but rather His Father's, to make that call.

Over the years I've had people who felt close to me ask for very sizable loans, and others have asked me if I would cosign for their loans. One couple asked if they could put us down as guardians over their children if they were killed in an accident or taken out by some tragic event. We were very flattered, but we really didn't want to raise more kids. We prayed hard for God's protection over that couple!

A third issue with John is that, if John feels someone has mistreated Jesus, he takes it very personally and gets ready to retaliate.

> *But they did not receive [Jesus], because His face was set for the journey to Jerusalem. And when His disciples James and John saw this, they said, "Lord, do You want us to command fire to come down from heaven and consume them, just as Elijah did?"*
>
> *But He turned and rebuked them, and said, "You do not know what manner of spirit you are of. For the Son of Man did not come to destroy men's lives but to save them." And they went to another village. (Luke 9:53-56)*

Most pastors have members like John who take it very personally when someone mistreats their pastor. They might even consider calling fire down from heaven on the offenders, if they thought they could! I've seen the time when it would have been nice to give them a Taser and orders to Tase anyone who says a negative word about their pastor. Just kidding!

The truth is, even the disciples who love you dearly will have their faults and flaws. And just think: if making disciples were easy, or if they could make themselves, they wouldn't need you. Jesus spent a lot of time in prayer and perhaps a good portion of it was spent talking to His Father about Pete's strong will or Judas's hurtful betrayal, or asking for wisdom on how to help Thomas overcome his doubt. One thing we do know: He never stopped loving them.

The Moral Majority

The Bible doesn't say much about the other disciples Jesus led. Most of them probably just tried to follow the best they knew how. And I don't know about your church, but my church is pretty much like Jesus's twelve: we have a few strong-willed; we've had a few betrayers, a few doubters, and a few who seem to love me unconditionally. And the rest just go along with whatever the leadership decides.

Make Disciples—But Don't Get Caught Up in Numbers

The purpose of the church is to make disciples, but as I said it's hard work. Jesus hand-picked twelve men whom He would disciple, and after three years, one swore that he didn't know who Jesus was, one sold him out, and one never stopped doubting. And this was the fruit that was produced under a leader who never sinned! So stop being so hard on yourself.

Though it's hard work, making disciples can be very fulfilling, especially if you are making disciples as you live out your sweet spot. Jesus is our ultimate role model and He lived out His ministry in His sweet spot. Jesus trained twelve as He traveled around the country doing what He was called to do: preaching the gospel and delivering the suffering and depraved. That was Jesus's sweet spot. He didn't run a discipleship school for the masses in Jerusalem, nor did He run a food bank for the hungry. We can be quite certain that there were many who needed Bible training and many who needed to be fed—but it wasn't going to be done by Jesus. Jesus was pastor to twelve. Jesus's God-honoring, disciple making number was twelve, and His calling was to preach the word, deliver hurting and depraved and with that God shouted from the heavens, "This is My beloved Son, in whom I am well pleased!" (Matthew 17:5).

Listen, pastors and church leaders: the guilt of not having more numbers on the roll has gone on long enough. So assemble your number (whether it's 2, 10, 30, 100, 500, or more) and settle into your sweet spot—*your* specific calling, not someone else's. Give God your best and listen to Him say, "This is My beloved pastor and church, in whom I am well pleased!"

Healthy Church

A few years ago, one of the newly elected bishops in our denomination made this statement to his pastors and leaders: "We are trying to figure out how to evaluate our churches other than just counting nickels and noses." When I heard that statement I knew in my heart of hearts that this newly elected bishop was onto something that the Holy Spirit was wanting to give the body of Christ. We have put so much emphasis on nickels and noses that we have lost focus on love and relationships, which are the key to making disciples.

It has been my experience that a good number of pastors seem to be feeling increasing pressure from their bishops, superintendents, Christian universities, and other overseers to grow numerically. I believe God is calling us to change from focusing on numerical growth to focusing on becoming a healthy church. This has been life-changing for me and for my church, because we no longer carry a false sense of guilt or stress over becoming larger. We focus on living in God's will in our personal lives and as a church, and that is so fulfilling. When we are healthy, that's when we are most effective in helping and reaching others.

The Mega Church Model

Some of our denominations and Christian universities have created a culture of "bigger is better" by bringing in mega church pastors and leaders and setting them up as the model or pattern to follow. It is not spoken, but it seems as though the consensus is that mega church is the way church should be done, and if you practice the principles set forth by the mega church you will reap a mega harvest. And that would probably be true, if we had the gifts and calling the mega church pastor has.

When I was pursing my Bachelor's and Master's I can't recall how many classes I sat in where a mega church pastor or a mega church consultant would come in and unveil some church growth strategy which had produced great fruit for their church. I'm sure God gave that strategy to them, so it worked for them, but it left many of us in the class feeling excited about all the possibilities and a little overwhelmed. (For some of us it was more than a little overwhelmed!)

The mega church seminars and workshops could be compared to bringing in Bill Gates or Warren Buffet in to teach mom-and-pop store owners how to improve their bottom line. The small store owners could probably learn some things that might help, but one has to wonder how relevant and applicable their training would be.

I believe the mom-and-pop store owners are a lot like small church pastors, in that God ordained them to run a small business that provides a good service for their communities. And I don't think I'm alone in saying, I *like* the mom-and-pop store atmosphere and I don't want them to change the way they do business. Many of us like to go into a store where they know us and can call us by name, instead of by a number. We like the personal treatment we get, and we like knowing that the store owner is one of us. We like knowing that they live their lives in our community, and we like the fact that we can build a personal relationship with the owners. The owner isn't a Sam Walton who we have heard of, but rather a friend we know and trust. The small church is like a mom-and-pop store; it offers a God-honoring service to its parishioners and communities, while building lifelong relationships. And I know I will receive some criticism that I just want my church to be a social club, and that might be true if God had given me the capacity to grow our church a lot larger than it is—but He didn't. So, I choose to enjoy the blessings of the size church that God gave me the ability to pastor.

Small business, small church; mega business, mega church—they are not right or wrong, they are *different*. And it is not right or wrong to be able to know most of the people you worship with or to know only a few people you worship with. It's not right or wrong to have complete access to your pastor or very little access to your pastor—but it is very different. I believe it takes very different pastors to operate such diversity in the kingdom of God, and that is the beauty that we should celebrate.

The gap between Warren Buffet and a mom-and-pop store, and between the small church and the mega church, is enormous—not better or worse, but still enormous. Here's something I found interesting: if you were to compare the number of employees in a small business to the number of members in the small church, small churches fare pretty well. In the business world, the average business employs 16.1 persons,[x] while the average church pastor oversees four or five times more than that in their church. And small business owners have a paycheck to motivate their employees, while most of the workforce in the small churches are volunteers. For anyone who thinks that having a paycheck to motivate the people who work for you doesn't matter, go out and recruit seventy volunteers and organize them into several different departmental tasks for the greater good of your mission. Ask them to give 10 percent of their income to your cause, and to give up one of their days off, and see how easy it is! And for all of you pastors who do this week after week, I celebrate you and thank God for you!

The church is not a business but there is a business side to the church, and in the small church many times the pastor is ultimately responsible for overseeing it. Most small churches that I know run a pretty tight budget and have a balancing act of bills, payroll, department needs, giving to missions, and more.

Consider this: if you have a small business with sixteen employees that is serving your community with a good product and good service, wouldn't you consider that business a blessing and a success? So why do we not consider a small church successful if its members are preaching and teaching the word of God, making disciples, loving their neighbors, and giving back to their communities and other parts of the world? Part of the answer may be that we are too stressed about not being able to add more numbers to our church roll. Some of us have tried so many growth strategies, without much success, we have become cynical of any outreach strategy. But what I found to be true for our church is that we didn't need another outreach strategy. We do practice an outreach Jesus used: loving people right where they are, and doing life and inviting others to do it with us. As we learn to live life and live it more abundantly, we find others who want to join us. Our church may not reach the masses, but we are reaching out with love to our neighbors.

Buying Mega Churches' Materials Doesn't Make You a Mega Church

I spent many years thinking our church would or should be a large church. Now, it's certainly honorable to want to make disciples, if making disciples is our real motive. I can only speak for myself, but my motive for wanting to double our church attendance wasn't always purely for the sake of souls. Some of my motives grew out of attending mega church conferences and thinking, "That's awesome, I should be doing something like that!" And part of my reason for wanting to double or quadruple was to prove to myself and others that I was as capable as the pastor with the big church. Don't get me wrong, I get very excited when I see another person or family come to Christ, but what I'm talking about is, I was more occupied with church growth strategies than I was with just loving people and doing life with them. For the small church, I believe, doing life with them is a huge part of developing them as disciples. And if that sounds like a small church way of living, that's because it is.

For me and for many of the pastors I know—pastors who have gone to many church growth conferences and purchased more church growth materials than we could possibly remember—there is one missing ingredient that we truly needed to convert our small church into a mega church—namely, the person who created these church growth materials. If we could have purchased the mega church pastor and brought him home with us and put him in charge, I'm quite sure he could have created another mega church at our church. Now, I'm being facetious; however, there is a lot of truth in that statement. Remember, 94 percent of all churches have average attendance of less than 500. Give this 94 percent all the latest and greatest church growth materials available and they will still reach the size encoded in *their* DNA, not the mega church pastor's DNA.

The fact is that the mega churches are the 1 percent who have the ability to grow and grow and grow. These churches have leaders who have been given the gifts and talents it takes to oversee a large staff, and who can attract the resources that are needed to hire more staff. The small church pastor can't buy that; it is a gift from God. We seem to think we can, so we go and purchase the mega churches' growth plans and outreach strategies and try to duplicate, to some degree, what the mega church has done. But it never seems to work.

What I have learned is to appreciate the gifts and talents God gave *me,* and I hope you appreciate the gifts and talents God gave you and what they produce for the kingdom of God. I believe that when we use our gifts to the best of our abilities, our churches will reach their God-honoring potential.

Affirmation versus Information

I believe part of the problem pastors have in accepting the realities of church growth comes, at least partially, from conferences, seminars, and church growth events. For example, in many of the church growth conferences I have attended, the majority of the teaching comes from mega church pastors, while the majority in attendance are pastors from significantly smaller churches.

The 1 percent mega church seems to be where most of the modeling and teaching for the small church comes from. While we can and do learn some principles or lessons from the mega pastors, more often than not when I have returned home after attending one of their conferences, I have come home with a head full of ideas that in reality were not very helpful to our church.

The problem isn't that it wasn't great material; the problem was it wasn't where my church and I were. Each church is unique and, although our gospel message is always the same, our assignments are as different as the pastors and members who make up each local church. I'm a leader; I love reading leadership books, listening to leadership CDs, and going to leadership events, and I love teaching leadership—and the fruit of that is that our church has good leaders. They are faithful, they love what they do, and they edify the church in their respective ministries. But to be honest, our church has not produced a lot of fruit from the materials we have purchased from other churches. Most of our fruit comes as we live out the Holy Bible in our everyday lives, simply sharing Jesus from who we are.

What I have experienced and found to be true of some of my pastor friends is that we have accumulated file cabinets filled with outreach or church growth strategies that we've picked up over the last several years, but those materials weren't what we had hoped for. Over the past twenty-five years I can remember on several occasions buying the latest, cutting-edge church growth material and feeling like once we initiated this material our church would break all kinds of growth records. And after a few months, I would realize that this wasn't the breakthrough material we had hoped for.

I'm not bashing conferences, seminars, or church growth workshops; in fact, I still enjoy attending and speaking at these events. What I am saying is this: I no longer allow others to saddle me, or my church, with their latest church growth strategies. Their strategies and growth plans work for them, because that is who they are. And it works for them because that is what God is doing through them. And it works for them because that is who God called them to reach. And it works for them because it is God's time for them to plant these particular seeds, or invest in this particular area. Now, if most of these same things line up with what God is doing in your life and church, then this material might be the fit you are looking for. But if God's plans for your church are different from His plans for their church, then even the best materials won't cause your church to achieve what their church has.

I believe the key thing to consider when attending any kind of leadership or church growth conference is this: any materials we purchase should affirm or confirm what God is already doing or prompting us to do. This helped me, and maybe it will do the same for you. I now go to leadership and church growth events looking not for information but for affirmation and confirmation. I have bought into too many "latest and greatest" church growth strategies that really didn't fit us, and cost us money and energy with little impact. Again, that was my fault, and not the fault of the church that was selling the strategy that had worked for them. However, I did learn from the experience.

I now attend conferences to glean something that might enhance what God is having us do and be. And that is probably what our mega church pastors and leaders intended in the first place. My problem was that I would go and hear some gifted speaker cast a compelling vision of how this strategy worked for his church, and the numbers it had produced for them, and how simple it was, and I would buy into it and off I would go. If you identify with what I am saying, then I want to challenge you to tweak your perspective before you attend your next church growth conference. And yes, I still believe we need to attend leadership and church growth conferences—

but before you go, pastor and leader, you need to clarify the direction God is taking you and your church, and have some sort of idea of what kinds of materials might be helpful to you and your church before you attend. If some new materials they offer will enhance what God is doing right now, it might be worth the time and expense to purchase them, but if it would be something you would have to take home and initiate, then you might want to spend some time praying about it before you buy it. It might also be good to answer this question before you go: Why am I going to this particular event? For me, I enjoy hearing what God is doing with other pastors and their congregations. I no longer go looking for answers to why we can't grow, or trying to figure out why we can't break some numerical barrier. I now go looking to sharpen how we might do the things we feel God has instructed us to do and pick up something that might help us do them better. In the past I would go to most conferences looking intently to find the holy grail of numerical growth, and then I would purchase "it" and leave the conference feeling like I was wearing Saul's armor. Now I go to conferences happy, because I know in my heart we are a healthy, Acts-two church that is living out God's will. I leave conferences happy now, and so can you.

Free Yourself from Guilt

I expect I will receive criticism from some of you who are thinking that bigger numbers means more souls saved. I get that, I really do, and I'm for winning all the souls we can—but what God has called me to address is this guilt and pressure to grow to a number to which God has not ordained us to grow.

God wants to set us free from condemnation and guilt from lack of numbers. And God wants to set us free from our need to apologize for our size. He wants to set us free from feeling like we have to try someone else's proven method of church growth instead of being who God created us to be. Instead of feeling guilty, let's celebrate each person God has added and will add to our church. Let's celebrate who they are and celebrate their gifts and purpose. Let's celebrate the vision and calling God gave us. Let's celebrate what we are able to contribute to our community and to other parts of the world. Our church has gotten pretty good at celebrating meeting the needs of widows, orphans, the hungry and the thirsty, whom God has given us the calling and resources to house, feed and give water. And we celebrate that we are an Acts-two church that participates in the teaching of God's word, fellowship, breaking of bread, outreach, and prayer!

The Alarming Facts on Pastor Burnout

I'm going to share some disturbing statistics concerning pastors, but before you read them I want to remind you that we do not have to be a part of these statistics. In John 10:10 Jesus said, "The thief does not come except to steal, and to kill, and to destroy. I have come that they may have life, and that they may have it more abundantly." And the truth is, what we have in Christ is enough to live life and live it more abundantly—but we have to choose to take hold of what He has given us and live it.

I believe there are too many pastors trying to live out someone else's life. They get caught up in someone else's vision and what God is doing in someone else's church that is growing. It's hard trying to be someone else. I know that to be true, because as I mentioned earlier, I did that for years.

Another thing that can quickly lead pastors away from being who God created them be is trying to please all of the church members. This is especially true in a small church. The pastor gets involved in too many areas and tries to take care of too many needs, because he or she doesn't want to disappoint anyone—a disappointed member might leave. When a church is small, sometimes the pastor will put up with a lot of abuse in order to keep the peace so no one leaves. There can be a fear that the needs and obligations of the church won't be met if someone leaves. That is bondage, and God did not call us to live there. The statistics you are about to read are to some degree proof of that.

As you read through these statistics, be honest as to where you are in each of these areas. Remember, the truth shall set you free. I'm convinced that these statistics represent pastors who are no longer living on the path God laid out for them, and the road to recovery starts with truth! If some of these statistics mirror your life, put a check mark by them. In the next chapter we will be talking about living in your sweet spot, which is where your values, gifts, talents, and passions line up with your daily life. And that is a great place to live. In fact, it is a place where, rather than facing stress and burnout, you will live life and live it more abundantly.

Pastor Burnout by the Numbers

According to the *New York Times*, "Members of the clergy now suffer from obesity, hypertension and depression at rates higher than most Americans.

In the last decade, their use of antidepressants has risen, while their life expectancy has fallen. Many would change jobs if they could."[xi]

The book *Pastors at Greater Risk* paints a bleak picture of America's clergy. Based on the Fuller Institute of Church Growth's 1991 Survey of Pastors, the book reports that:

- *90% of pastors work more than 46 hours a week.*

- *90% felt they were inadequately trained to cope with ministry demands.*

- *50% feel unable to meet the needs of the job.*

- *70% say they have a lower self esteem now than when they started out.*

- *75% of pastors reported a significant stress-related crisis at least once in their ministry.*

- *A45% of pastors say that they've experienced depression or burnout to the extent that they needed to take a leave of absence from ministry.*

- *40% reported a serious conflict with a parishioner at least once a month, and 37% confessed having been involved in inappropriate sexual behavior with someone in the church.*

The clergy has the second highest divorce rate among all professions. 80% of pastors say they have insufficient time with spouse. 80% believe that pastoral ministry has affected their families negatively; 52% say they and their spouses believe that being in pastoral ministry is hazardous to their family's well-being and health; and 33% say that being in ministry was an outright hazard to their family.

70% of pastors do not have someone they consider a close friend. 56% of pastors' wives say that they have no close friends.

And more bleak statistics the book quotes from an article on pastors' families:

- 94% of pastors feel pressured to have an ideal family.

- The top six problems in clergy marriages are: 81%, insufficient time; 71%, use of money; 70%, income level; 64%, communication difficulties; 63%, congregational expectations; and 57%, differences over leisure.

- 24% have received or are receiving martial counseling.

- 33% of pastors are dissatisfied with the level of sexual intimacy in their marriages; and pastors report 16% of their spouses are dissatisfied, which 69% blame on their busy schedule and 35% on frequent night church meetings.

- 22% seek supplemental income to make ends meet.

- 28% feel current compensation is inadequate.

- 69% of the spouses work outside the home to make ends meet.

- 67% of the pastors feel positive about their spouses working outside their home.

- *9% of clergy have had extramarital affairs.*

- *19% have had inappropriate sexual contact with another person other than their spouse.*

- *55% of clergy have no one with whom they can discuss their sexual temptations.*

These statistics take their toll on pastors. According to pastoralcareinc.com "Over 1,700 pastors left the ministry every month last year." And, according to Dr. Archibald Hart, a psychology professor at Fuller Theological Seminary, "Doctors, lawyers and clergy have the most problems with drug abuse, alcoholism, and suicide."[xii]

As leaders, we must take responsibility for our actions. As leaders, we have to get the focus back on health instead of numbers, or we will continue to stress and overextend ourselves. A healthy church starts with creating healthy leaders, and creating healthy leaders starts with creating a healthy senior pastor. The good news is, once the senior pastor begins to practice a healthy lifestyle, his family and his church are likely to follow suit. I realize that your family and church are free moral agents and your being healthy doesn't guarantee either will follow, but an unhealthy pastor is much more likely to produce unhealthy followers.

Listen, pastor and leaders: God gave us our families to share life with and enjoy. And He gave us our churches to lead and love, but He didn't give us our churches so we could play superpastor—able to meet every need in a single bound. I imagine if Jethro had had some statistics similar to ones I shared with you, he would have brought them to the meeting that he had with Moses when Moses had overextended himself. And, as Jethro went through the stats, Moses would have been shaking his head and saying, "Yep, that sound like me," or "That sounds like where I'm headed!"

If some of these stats describe you, just remember: *you* are the one who has to fix it. And God will give you the wisdom and strength you need to get your life in order. Let me share a few things that have been a great help to me.

Let Go of Unrealistic Expectations

Accepting our limitations can be a real ego crusher. I know firsthand, because I thought for more than twenty years our church would someday take a huge leap in growth once we had the right strategy, the right persons on board, or the right *something*. And I found out that I am not alone.

I did a personal survey of a few pastors from different denominations, and this what I found. The pastors were in their fifties and sixties; all had been the senior pastors of their churches for between ten and thirty years; their church attendance was between 50 and 150. What was interesting, but not very realistic, was that these pastors said that they believed that their attendance would double or quadruple in the next five to ten years. None of them had experienced a significant increase in numbers in the past several years, but in spite of this fact, they were hoping for and believing in huge increases in attendance.

So what would cause these seasoned pastors to expect such an increase in numbers, when they had no significant proof from past growth? I believe a lot of it has to do with our church culture: it's still all about counting nickels and noses. Numerical growth and bigger buildings is how we now evaluate our churches' success. So, it would make sense that numerical growth is how the average pastor judges success or failure.

These pastors also said they feel pressured to grow numerically. I believe there is such a thing as a godly sense of pressure, prompting us to reach out with love and light—but it is not a hopeless sense that plants condemning questions in our hearts and minds such as, "What's wrong with us, why can't we grow our church?"

If you have tried and tried to break some numerical barrier without success and are feeling like something is wrong with you, I would like you to consider giving it to God, who invites you to cast all of your cares on Him. Start placing your focus on growing a *healthy* church and let God take care of the increase.

Stop Comparing Numbers

Since average churches house the majority of Christians, it would make sense that the majority of the souls won, good deeds done, and money invested in ministry and missions come through the average church. I believe that God is just fine with that; the problem seems to be that pastors aren't.

We've all heard some very inspirational talks by mega church pastors on how they added 500 or more in one outreach campaign, and those kinds of stats can be very intimidating to a small church pastor. I'm sitting there thinking, "This pastor has accumulated more members with this one outreach than I've been able to reach in my entire years of ministry." Maybe you're a bigger person than I am, and when you hear those kinds of numbers you just get excited about the increase of souls for the kingdom. And that's where we all need to be: Romans 12:15, "Rejoice with those who rejoice." I actually experience both emotions; I get excitedly intimidated. However, I do give God the glory for any church reaching hundreds of people with the gospel. Go, God!

I agree that we should all reach out with the gospel until Jesus comes, but I don't agree that the majority of small churches have the ability to grow into large churches or mega churches. We pastors should continue to grow personally as church shepherds and leaders, going from milk to meat in areas we may need to mature in, but the statistics reveal that God has not given the majority of pastors the ability to grow a congregation larger than 499 members. If He has, then the vast majority of pastors in the USA are in trouble with God. But I don't believe that to be the case at all; I think God is proud of each church that lifts up the name of Jesus!

Focus on Health, not Size

The church I pastor no longer focuses on numbers or breaking numerical records; we now focus on being healthy. And it is so freeing! We are not lazy, nor are we a closed church that doesn't want to grow. In a normal year we have a few who receive Christ and are baptized, and we replace as many we lose (meaning that they move, die, or quit coming).

We do focus on making healthy disciples out of the ones who are attending. We do our best to feed and lead our flock and invest our time, talent, and treasure where we believe God is leading. And these things we highly value.

I have been the Senior Pastor of the same church for over twenty-five years. During that time I have few regrets, but one regret I do have is carrying around a false hope of reaching and maintaining a larger flock than God ordained me to shepherd. BUT NO MORE! Today I have no guilt, no false sense of having to break some numerical barrier. I truly believe that we are operating at or near our God-honoring potential and we are very excited about that.

I have leadership talents and like to offer them to organizations in our community. I'm a hospice volunteer; I visit those who are dying and shine light and hope into their finals days on earth. I'm also an extrovert and love socializing, so I participate in our homeowners' association and utilize my gifts by bringing leadership and community.

So, what resources and talents has God given you to share with your community, your world? Use them. Do mega ministry. It's huge to the person or persons who are receiving from you. And God is well pleased when we simply use the gifts He has given to us. It is mega to Him. The Bible teaches that, when you feed someone who is hungry, give a drink to those who don't have clean water, or visit a shut-in or those who are incarcerated, it is just like you are feeding, giving water to, or visiting God. And that is mega ministry!

Trust that God Has Put You in the Right Place

One has to wonder if the leaders in Moses's camp had the same sorts of stresses as pastors today when Moses assigned them to help judge the people: "Moreover you shall select from all the people able men, such as fear God, men of truth, hating covetousness; and place such over them to be rulers of thousands, rulers of hundreds, rulers of fifties, and rulers of tens" (Exodus 18:21).

Each leader was held to the same standard—able, God-fearing men of truth who hate covetousness—and the same can be said for a pastor today who oversees ten or ten thousand. Biblical standards don't change with the size of the church. The standard for ruling thousands and the standard for ruling ten are one and the same.

So, what *does* change? The difference might be found in the word "able." God has given each of us gifts, talents, and abilities to fulfill our calling, whether it is pastoring ten or ten thousand. What I have noticed is this: the small church, medium church, large church, and mega church are each led by men and women who have the calling and ability to lead them. I know that that is a overly simple statement, but we all need to reminded once in a while that God is proud of us right where we are. We don't need to break another attendance record or stress over building a bigger building in order to be on God's "A" list. In fact, for some of you who have been feeling like you have to add more people, more services, more buildings, the truth may be that you need to do *less*—less for the church, and more for yourself and your family. You may need to put fun on your schedule, family on your schedule, and more "you time" on your schedule.

Sweaty Palms on the Playground

When Moses chose his leaders, one has to wonder if his leaders felt a lot like we did when we were kids standing on the playground all lined up and being picked one by one for sports teams. Did the leaders who were picked to lead hundreds think, "If Moses had any discernment at all he would have picked me to lead thousands!"? And how about the guys who were picked to oversee groups of tens—do you think these leaders felt like the kids who were picked last on the playground? Can you imagine some of the conversations going on as these leaders went home and told their spouses that Moses had chosen them to lead? "And how many did Moses pick you to lead?" asks the inquiring spouse. "Ah, only ten, but it was a big deal just to be picked," replies the leader. That is purely speculation on my part; my hope is that each leader was feeling humbled and privileged that God had picked them to lead His people. And that's the way you and I should feel about God choosing us to lead a part of the body of Christ, regardless of the size of our group.

Chosen

Moses's leaders were chosen for their leadership positions; they didn't get to pick their leadership roles. Listen, pastors and leaders: God chose us to do what we do. He gave us the ability to oversee the flock we shepherd, and we should be humbled and take pride in the fact that God chose us to lead a part of His family. God has picked you to lead your church and has given you all the gifts you need to lead it. Whether He chose you to lead thousands, hundreds, fifties, or tens, He knows where you belong and where it is that you fit best.

Here's something else we need to remember when it comes to a church's size: God also chooses *members*, according to each one's own ability to serve in different size churches. God's calling and gifting on your life has a direct effect on the people

God will assign to your church. Their gifts and abilities fit under your leadership. They are allowed to grow and use their gifts under your supervision. I heard a pastor giving a testimony about being hired by a church of a thousand. He said that the church had been at a thousand for many years under the founding pastor. When he took over as senior pastor he begin to grow the church, but most of the former leaders who had been on staff there for years were fired because they didn't have the ability to help lead more than one thousand. These leaders who helped build a church of a thousand found themselves a mismatch with their new leader. Some of them probably felt like failures for a season because they weren't equipped to help lead a church of more than one thousand. In some cases, in the name of church growth, we treat church more like a business than like a church. I will never forget getting acquainted with a group of young leaders at a leadership event who were very stressed about losing their ministry positions because they weren't sure whether they were going to hit the required number of new converts they were expected to add to the church. For their church, it was hit the numbers or hit the road.

What I want you to see is this: your church size is as much about the people you serve and their gifts, talents, and abilities as it is about *your* gifts, talents, and abilities. When you accepted the call to lead your church, you also made it possible for others in the body, who have gifts and talents that fit your vision, to serve. The church you pastor is not too big or too small for them; it is just right. Your church provides a place where the people in your town or community can come and feel like they belong, where they can come and serve and feel that they matter. They attend your church because they identify with you and what your church offers.

Discovering and Living in Your Sweet Spot

What is a sweet spot? We hear golfers talk about the sweet spot on a golf club. It's a very small area in the center of the club that delivers maximum performance. When you hit the ball from the sweet spot, the ball will usually go farther and straighter, producing a great shot.

The same could be said about *your* sweet spot. It is the place in your daily agenda where you are allowed to operate from your gifts and strengths, doing what you love to do. When that connection is made, it is sweet. It is getting to do what you were born to do.When you are operating from your sweet spot you are operating from who you are. That's where you fulfill your God-ordained purpose. That's where you find and experience significance. When you are operating in it you are faster and stronger, you are hitting on all cylinders, your energy level is at its peak, your soul is getting fed, and you are thinking, "This is what I was born to do!"

I have discovered that the more clearly you define your sweet spot, the more likely you are to operate in it. Life can get hectic and busy, and if you haven't defined your sweet spot, you can drift off course and wind up spending way too much time doing things you shouldn't be doing. And as you drift out of your sweet spot, life can become very draining.

As a life coach, I often help clients who feel stuck to discover they have drifted off course and are working outside of their sweet spot. Most of the time when I ask why they are doing what they are doing, it is the same answer: "Because it needs to be done," or "If I don't do it, it won't get done." As pastors we can wear many hats, depending on the needs of the people we serve. Even in a small church there are all kinds of legitimate needs that can pull at us and lead us away from operating in our sweet spot. As a rule, this is what our church practices: if God wants us to meet certain needs, He will provide the leadership and resources. If He doesn't, it's probably okay not to provide that service or ministry.

I do understand that sometimes leading a church will require us to do certain things outside our gifts and strengths. Hopefully, when it does, it will only take a minimal amount of our time, and we should only allow it to be for a season. Working outside their gifts, strengths, and passions will at least contribute to the fact that so many pastors walk away from the ministry.

Identifying Your Sweet Spot

If you haven't been able to define your sweet spot, maybe this will help. In my coaching business, I take life coach trainees and clients who are scattered or stuck through a module called Life Focus. They look at the ten life categories: Spiritual Life, Marriage/Single, Family Life/Children, Work/Job, Church/Ministry, Financial, Physical Stewardship, Personal Development, Social Stewardship, and Hobbies/Recreation. I have them set short-term and long-term goals in each area.

I think most North Americans don't do enough reflecting. We are so caught up in what needs to be done right now, we get lost in the immediate. Taking time to reflect and align our future according to our values, gifts, strengths, and passions is a powerful way to live life. Living these ten life categories with intention and purpose plays a huge role in living in your sweet spot, or as Jesus called it, abundant life. Reflecting on these ten areas and taking time to sort through them and write out some short-term and long-term goals will help you figure out what is most important to you. And whatever is most important to you is what you value. Defining what you value will enable you to see if what you say you value is indeed where you are living. Living out your values is how you operate in your sweet spot.

When I worked through Life Focus as a coach trainee, here's what I came away with. First, my sweet spot is developing others and helping them find *their* sweet spot. Helping others discover and live in their sweet spot is a huge high for me. At the church I pastor we have eighteen department leaders, all of whom are volunteers. Yet we have very little turnover in our leadership positions. I think the main reason for such low turnover is that we try to make sure that our leaders are in their sweet spot. If people love what they do, they will stay in position for long periods of time.

My second discovery—and this hit on two of my values, family and fitness—was that I love taking walks with Jana, my wife, in the sunshine. After work my wife and I walk and debrief each other about our day. We cherish that time so much. And the days when the weather permits, which includes anything under 100 degrees in the summer or over 40 degrees in the winter, it is an added bonus to walk outside in the sunshine. I wish I could get across to you how powerfully these two simple things have helped me stay focused. I know they sound so simple, but being able to articulate my values and walk them out every day of my life has enriched my life, my marriage, and my ministry in such a powerful way. It is good to be me!

Another thing I discovered was, when I wrote out my values and began to align my life with them, my energy level increased. Why? Because I'm living life out of who God created me to be. My life is more about *being* than it is about *doing*. I now understand why God said, "I am who I am" and not "I do what I do."

Once I could verbalize my sweet spot, I stopped doing a lot of little things that others could do, and cut some ministries that we didn't have leaders for. We develop good leaders, and by "good" I mean leaders who are fulfilled and producing fruit. They love what they do and are very gifted at what they do. And because of that, they experience success and significance.

Operating in Your Sweet Spot is Life-Giving

Here's some good news: I have discovered that when people operate from their sweet spot, they can do less and accomplish more. Yeah! Think about it; it takes a lot less energy to do something that you are very good at than it does to do something that you are not very good at. For example, I'm not very knowledgeable at doing things on the computer. So, when I want to share something with the congregation on the overhead screen in our sanctuary, I make a call and it happens. The computer techs appreciate the chance to use (and maybe even show off) their skills and I get to share my vision with the congregation. I do the vision casting; the techs do the visual effects; the congregation is exposed to the vision. When everyone is contributing from their sweet spots, it a lot like the TV commercial where people have an "easy button" for things that need to be done. When they push it, you hear a voice say, "That was easy." Jesus lived in His sweet spot, and He said His yoke was easy and His burdens were light.

Operating in your sweet spot may be physically demanding at times, but I believe that most of the things you do inside of your sweet spot are emotionally and mentally life-giving or energizing. A good example of that is the time when Jesus is in a crowd where the faith is high and every person He touches is getting healed; three days later He's still going. Jesus and the crowd are physically exhausted, so much so that Jesus instructs His disciples to set the people down and feed them so they don't pass out from hunger on their way back home. That must have been one of Jesus's most life-giving days on Planet Earth.

Defining Your Purpose Will help in Defining Your Sweet Spot

Jesus clearly knew His purpose and in that purpose is where He lived everyday. He was very adamant about following God's will and setting boundaries for His life and ministry: "Then Jesus said to them, '… I do nothing of Myself; but as My Father taught Me, I speak these things. And He who sent Me is with Me. The Father has not left Me alone, for I always do those things that please Him" (John 8:28-29).

Jesus didn't plant churches, He didn't have a school of ministry, and He didn't build a mega church. He chose and led twelve. He invested Himself in twelve. If Jesus came to earth today and wanted to invest three years in twelve more disciples before His final return, I wonder how the church, as a whole, would look at that?

Jesus's life was a great example of what living in your sweet spot looks like. He identified His sweet spot with what was written in Scripture, and you and I should be able to do the same. For example, let's look back at Luke 4:18-21:

"The Spirit of the Lord is upon Me,

Because He has anointed Me

To preach the gospel to the poor;

He has sent Me to heal the brokenhearted,

To preach deliverance to the captives

And recovery of sight to the blind,

To set at liberty those who are oppressed;

To proclaim the acceptable year of the Lord."

Then He closed the book, and gave it back to the attendant and sat down. And the eyes of all who were in the synagogue were fixed on Him. And He began to say to them, "Today this Scripture is fulfilled in your hearing."

Jesus was saying to the congregation that day, "The person in that scripture is *me*. This is what I have been called to do. This is what I was born to do. This is what I will give My life to!" And that's what He did. He defined His calling and then lived it.

So which verses do you see in Scripture that you feel you could stand up and read before your congregation this Sunday and then close the book and say, "And that, ladies and gentlemen, describes me to a T! That is my calling, my sweet spot, and I will devote the rest of my life to it!"

For example, I could use Romans 12:8 (NLT): "If God has given you leadership ability, take the responsibility seriously." If I were reading that to my church this Sunday I could close the book and say, "Today I want you to know that I am the person to whom God gave leadership responsibility. I take leadership very seriously, because leadership is the instrument that God gave me to play, and as long as I have the privilege of leading something I will be fulfilled and produce fruit." I have functioned as a leader for most of my adult life; I am presently in a leadership role as a senior pastor, a business owner, and a certified life coach/life coach trainer; all of my gift tests point to leadership; and my friends and colleagues confirm that I am called to leadership. And, to fine-tune that a little further, as a leader I love to help leaders, teams, and organizations discover and operate in their sweet spots.

So which verse in the Bible describes you? What do your past, present, gifts test, friends and colleagues say your dominant gifts are? If you're not sure, reflect on your past and present. Take some gifts test. Ask your friends and colleagues.

If you already know what your gifts are, then all you need to do is keep yourself in position so that you can operate in your gifts. Operating in your gifts, strengths, and passions is operating in your sweet spot. Operating in your gifts will bring fruit and fulfillment to your life. Working within your gifts and calling, and giving it everything you have, may be tiring and hard work, but I don't believe you will ever burn out because you will be doing what you love.

One caution I would give is this: when you are doing the things you were created to do, it can be so exciting that you can neglect other things that also need to be taken care of. That's why it is important to have goals written out in your ten life categories, not just one.

Living Out Your Values

Earlier I mentioned how identifying and living out your values is living in your sweet spot; let's take a closer look at that. We all have a set of values that run our lives. Whether we can verbalize them or not, we do what we do—and do *not* do what we do *not* do—based on our values. For example, let's say honesty is one of your values. If you hand the cashier at a restaurant a ten dollar bill and she gives you change for a twenty, you won't hesitate to correct her right then and there. But if you put the extra money in your pocket and consider it the cashier's mistake and your gain, then you *don't* value honesty, you only *say* you value honesty.

As a life coach I often deal with the issue of people saying they value one thing and living another. For instance, someone will say "I value health" but the reality is that they are overweight and out of shape and do very little (if anything) to promote their health. Another commonly stated value is family, but as the *Pastors at Greater Risk* stats revealed, many pastors have a hard time living out their values when it comes to their families. When it comes to a healthy family life, common obstacles for pastors include: working long hours, juggling twenty ministry plates at once, being addicted to ego strokes, fearing losing momentum, or a dozen other things. If family is indeed high on the priority list, then the time they take up on the daily planner should reflect that.

That's why I believe that it is so important to list your top four or five values. The benefit in being able to clearly identify your values is that, when life pulls you off-course, you can quickly identify that that's what's happening. For example, my values are: faith, family, friends, fitness, and fun. I pretty much live these out every day. I realize that faith may seem like a broad statement, but my walk of faith is narrowed down to what that looks like to me—walking it out in a balance that fits me, my calling, my family, and our church. Naming fitness as a value helps me stay conscious of working out and considering the portion sizes of what I eat. And, whether I am at home or out of town in a hotel somewhere, I exercise and watch my portions. Just to let you know, I'm not sporting a six-pack, but I do try to maintain a healthy body.

Just remember: if you write out your values and there's no evidence in your life of one or some of them being a value, you need to take another look at them.

Jesus Lived Out His Values

Jesus valued intimacy. As a result, He hand-picked twelve to disciple. He could have chosen a hundred or a thousand just as easily.

Jesus valued prayer. Jesus is found many times getting away from the crowds and spending time in prayer. Here's something Jesus taught us that is worth mentioning: Jesus had twelve disciples, but He didn't invite all twelve to join Him in His prayer times. I'm sure the other disciples were aware that Jesus and His inner circle were having these times together. And by the way, the Bible doesn't call Jesus's intimate prayer circle a clique. Jesus seems to value Peter, James, and John as a part of His prayer team, and I believe that it is healthy for pastors to have an inner circle who will pray in agreement and help them live out their values.

Jesus valued faith. Jesus never stressed over feeding thousands if it was time to eat, nor did He stress over lodging, paying taxes, or a ride if He needed one. He lived a life of faith before His disciples and was very transparent with all of them when they displayed a lack of faith.

Find your Sweet Spot in Giving

It's important to define your purpose and live out your values in your church's giving as well as its ministries. A few years ago, in a Sunday-morning prayer meeting that takes place in my office every week, our head elder said, "I believe the Lord is wanting us to finance a water well in Africa." Our intercessors and I spent some time praying and received confirmation, and that was a turning point for our church financially. Since then God has led us to build houses for widows in Guatemala, as well. We still do local missions, but our church is no longer a welfare department, giving to everyone who calls or comes by wanting a handout. We no longer support individuals whose needs were created by poor management, drugs, gambling, or quitting their jobs, and who were using our church as a welfare system. And the local missions we do give to are carefully screened. Here's the exciting part: as we've defined our missions more clearly, our giving to missions has increased and so has our general fund.

There is one other thing I want to mention on giving. At the beginning of each new year, since we revised our giving habits, we ask our intercessors to pray for God's direction on where we should be giving. God has directed us and challenged us, and our giving has become an exciting journey for our congregation. Getting our intercessors involved in our giving has also made them feel valued and it has allowed them to use their gift in an important area of ministry. They are now aware and know that they are an important part of our church being able to give more. It is very edifying for the intercessors and for our church.

Temptations to Leave Your Sweet Spot

The Pull of the Murmurs

It took a lot of thought and processing for me to discover and define my sweet spot, but now that I have, I fight hard to stay in it. As a leader I have discovered that people will consistently tell you what you "need" to do. I have an answer to all of the well-meaning people who come up to me and ask, "Pastor, do you know what you need to do?" I look them in the eye and politely say, "Why yes, I know exactly what I need to do, but thanks for checking!"

Hear me, pastors: I believe another part of why pastors are leaving the ministry at an alarming rate is that they are being pulled off-course by the wants and needs of their congregants. A pastor can get so scattered by chasing the wants and needs of the congregation that they find themselves doing ministry outside their gifts, strengths, and passions. Operating in your gifts, strengths, and passions is life-giving, while living outside of your gifts, strengths, and passions is life-draining. If what you are doing is sucking the life out of you, that is not a sustainable pace, and you will either burn out or walk away.

Sticking to your sweet spot may sometimes mean cutting back on a ministry or service that the church has offered in the past. Some church members may have a hard time with this, especially if the church has offered this service for quite some time. If they do, I ask them to step up and lead it or create a team to lead it. They may give me the "I'm not qualified" or a number of other excuses, but I remind them that they are the ones who have the burden for this ministry or service, and God has not called me to lead it. They can pray about leading it, pray that God will send someone in to lead it, or ask

God for peace to let it go, but I'm not leading anything that God has not called me to lead. And I let them know that I'm not going to ask them to lead things that are not in their sweet spot. We all may have to lead or help out in a ministry from time to time that is not in our sweet spot, but it should be established from the beginning that it is for a short season only.

It's good to remember that sometimes Jesus made people unhappy when he stuck to his sweet spot, too. Luke 19:7: "But when they saw it, they all murmured, saying, 'He has gone to be a guest with a man who is a sinner.'" The murmuring did not deter Jesus from going home with Zacchaeus; instead, Jesus affirmed His sweet spot by stating, "for the Son of Man has come to seek and to save that which was lost" (Luke 19:10). Regardless of who was unhappy about it, this is what Jesus was sent to do!

Listen, pastors and leaders: every once in a while, when the saints are murmuring, you may have to affirm your actions by reminding yourself: this is who I am, this is what I have been sent to do, and my calling is not about pleasing people.

If you feel like you are not operating out of our sweet spot, you might want to answer this question: "Am I doing things that please God, or am I doing things that please the church?" Every pastor is different, and each has been given different gifts, strengths, and passions. If we allow the church to pull us off course and spend a good amount of our time doing ministry outside our gifts, strengths, and passions, it will become very draining. Staying inside our gifts, strengths, and passions is where we receive energy and life.

More Needs than We Can Meet

One reason we need to be careful to define our mission is that there are more needs in the world than we can meet, and we need to figure out what to do when we run into a situation that is outside our calling. Jesus sometimes got pulled into situations outside his calling. At one point, Jesus is trying to hide out (we try to draw crowds; Jesus tried to escape from crowds!) but a Syrophoenician woman tracks him down like a bloodhound and will not shut up or back down until she gets what she wants from Him. First, Jesus ignores her. Then the disciples encourage Jesus to send her away, and finally Jesus makes this statement: "I was not sent except to the lost sheep of the house of Israel" (Matthew 15:24). It's almost as if this tenacious lady is deaf to anything but "Okay, I will heal your daughter!"

Jesus makes it quite clear that His calling is to Israelites and not Gentiles. But this lady isn't ducking her head and walking off, no, she continues her pursuit and worships Jesus. So, Jesus makes one last attempt to send her away: "It is not good to take the children's bread and throw it to the little dogs" (Matthew 15:26). One would think that that would be clear enough to send her on her way, but not this lady! She comes back with the statement that pulls Jesus off the Israeli track on to the Gentile track for a brief moment: "Yes, Lord, yet even the little dogs eat the crumbs which fall from their masters' table" (Matthew 15:27). One of Jesus's consistent rebukes to His own disciples was having little or no faith, and here this woman is displaying a ton of faith. After He grants her request and heals her daughter, I can imagine Jesus looking at His disciples and saying, "Now, that, my boys, is the kind of faith it takes to move mountains!"

So, what was it that pulled Jesus into this woman's situation, when He had already assured her that His call was not to Gentiles?

It was her faith. Jesus values and operates in a high level of faith. And when Jesus sees her larger-than-mustard-seed faith He can no longer resist this mother's request.

The same can be said of you. If someone around you has a need, and their solution lives within your gifts and abilities, whether you have the time or not, you will be drawn to it like a moth to a light or a bird dog near a quail or pheasant. I like to hunt quail and pheasant and love to watch a good bird-dog hunt. When they get close to a quail or pheasant the dogs get very intense and focused, and that's the way I get when I get around some setting where there is a need for leadership and no leader. All of my faculties stand at attention and I start zeroing in on the specific need. It doesn't matter whether the people there want me to provide leadership or not; I'm a leader, and I'm thinking, they need me and my gift. It's my leadership duty to offer assistance. I can't help it; I turn into "Leadership Man"! I hear the song begin to play: "There's no need to fear, leadership man is here!"

The problem is, there are way too many leadership needs in the world for "Leadership Man" to meet—and the same goes for you. There are more legitimate needs in the area of your gifts and passions than you have time to meet. I use the word "legitimate" because, as a pastor, when you see a need—especially when it's within your sphere of your ability and it's not being taken care of—you can feel a deep pull to take care of it. We have to stop and ask if this need fits in with the calling God has given us. Jesus had such faith that He could feed thousands at any given moment, but He didn't have a feeding program. And feeding the poor is something that is near and dear to God's heart. Just because there's a need and you are more than qualified to meet it, it doesn't mean that you should.

I think this is especially true when it comes to the needs of your church. As a pastor or leader, there are many things that you could do in your church and in your community, but what is it that God specifically called you to do? Think about it. Jesus wasn't being harsh towards this poor woman; He just knew that Gentiles, for the most part, weren't who He was called to minister to at this particular time. If you had been there the day Jesus and His disciples were trying their best to get rid of the Syrophoenician woman as she's begging for help, and you didn't have a clue who Jesus was, what would you have thought about Him and His crew? I can remember one of the first times I read this account as a baby Christian; I truly thought that Jesus must have been having a bad day. Of course, I now realize that Jesus was simply staying fixed on His sweet spot. Jesus's ultimate goal was to become the Savior of the world, but for now His focus was towards the children of Israel.

Man Your Sweet Spot

I believe with all of my heart that the local church is the hope of the world—but the local church is in trouble. There are too many small churches closing down, and pastors, we can't blame our church members. We are the leaders and God is going to hold us accountable. If we get healthy, our churches will be healthy. And the only way for pastors to be healthy is to start pleasing God, not people, and to operate out of our sweet spots. The good news is, when you please God and operate out of your sweet spot, God is pleased, you become a healthy pastor, and your church is placed in a position to become healthy.

As a small church pastor, I know some of the fears you can have about saying no to the wants and needs of persistent church members. Some may talk about you or call you lazy, and some may even quit the church. And I know that everyone wants the pastor to come see them when they are sick. Everyone wants the pastor to come to *their* meetings or to *their* events. Everyone wants the pastor to do *their* wedding, funeral, or baptism. And we love to please people, so we veer off our sweet spot and tread down the road of pleasing the masses. I have pastor friends who run themselves silly trying to meet all the needs of their church members. It's hard to schedule a lunch appointment with them, they are so busy! And most of the time they are drained, and are constantly talking about how busy they are.

I know how that is, because I used to do that too. But I have discovered that God has placed many people in our church who are willing to do the work of the ministry and who are so fulfilled in doing so, that I step back and let them use their gifts and talents for

God. That gives me time to lead, feed, and develop my church. So most of my time is spent on studying, preparing sermon series and Bible studies, and providing leadership within our church wherever it is needed. And that is life-giving to me, not life-draining.

Final Thoughts

My intent in writing this book was to bring some perspective to how we look at the small church. I'm convinced that my church has reached (or at least operates near) its God-honoring potential, and I hope that will be the same for many of you. I no longer entertain thoughts of "Why can't we grow?" and I no longer stress over church attendance numbers. I hope this, too, will be the case for many of you.

Being a healthy church, and being light and salt right where we are, is now the order of the day. As leaders, we must take responsibility for our actions. As leaders, we have to get the focus back on health instead of numbers, or we will continue to stress and overextend ourselves. God gave us our families to share life with and enjoy. And He gave us our churches to lead and love, but He didn't give us a church so we could play superpastor—able to meet every need in a single bound. Jethro came and gave Moses a much-needed talk about overextending himself, and for some of you who are putting way too many hours into trying to grow your church, let me be your Jethro. What you are doing is not good for you, your family, or your church. Find some men and women who are able, and let them help you carry your load.

I want to encourage you to find your sweet spot. Remember, your sweet spot is where you can do more in less time and the work will be energizing while you are doing it. Clearly define your values, the things that matter most to you and your family. Live them, guard them, and enjoy them. Be healthy, so you can reach your God-honoring potential. That's all God requires.

1. Random House Webster's Dictionary, 1999, s.v. "average."

"The Coast Redwood, Tallest Tree in the World, http://sunnyfortuna.com/explore/redwoods_facts.htm.

Jay Childs, "Church Growth vs. Church Seasons: Not every church is in the 'my, how you've grown' stage, and that's okay," *Christianity Today Leadership Journal* (Nov 29, 2010), accessed March 14, 2012. http://www.christianitytoday.com/le/2010/fall/churchgrowthseason.html.

Gary McIntosh, One Size Doesn't Fit All: Bringing Out the Best in Any Size Church (Grand Rapids: Revell, 1999), 17-18.

McIntosh, *One Size,* #.

: Thom S. Rainer, C. Peter Wagner, and Elmer L. Towns, *The Everychurch Guide to Growth: How Any Plateaued Church Can Grow* (Nashville: B&H Books, 1998), 135-136.

"Top 100 Largest Churches," *Outreach Magazine* (2008), http://www.sermoncentral.com/articleb.asp?article=Top-100-Largest-Churches.

"O Come All Ye Faithful," *The Economist* (Nov 1 2008), http://www.economist.com/node/10015239?story_id=10015239&CFID=25385374.

Unless otherwise noted, all Bible quotes are from the New King James Version.

x pafalafa-ga, "How Many Employees Does the Average US Company Have?". (Nov 23, 2003), http://answers.google.com/answers/threadview/id/279843.html.

Paul Vitello, "Taking a Break from the Lord's Work," *The New York Times* (August 1 2010), http://www.nytimes.com/2010/08/02/nyregion/02burnout.html.

xii Cited in Glenda F. Hodges and Harold B. Betton, *Spirituality and Medicine: Can the Two Walk Together?* (Bloomington, Ind.: AuthorHouse, 2008).

Made in the USA
Lexington, KY
01 August 2017